I0464234

THE ART OF WALL STREET INVESTING

BY
John Moody

The Art of Wall Street Investing
By
John Moody

Preface

ALTHOUGH the popular impression is probably the reverse, it is certainly a fact that a greater sum of money is annually lost in this country through unwise investment in Wall Street, than through pure speculation. While fortunes are daily jeopardized and dissipated through speculation in stocks, bonds, grain futures and like ventures, yet the many sums, large and small, which annually leave the pockets of actual investors are far greater in amount. Indeed, I would almost say that the losses incurred through "unwise Wall Street investing" are easily tenfold the losses occasioned through mere speculation on the exchanges.

And furthermore, the losses resulting from unwise investing are far more important to the community at large; for while speculative losses are in a sense anticipated, the losses through mistaken investments are usually unexpected and unprepared for. Speculative losses often represent the

The Art of Wall Street Investing
By
John Moody

loss of money easily gained, either through former speculations or from other sources, but the average loss of the investing public is generally a loss of hard- earned or industriously accumulated savings; and therefore such losses are felt more deeply by the community.

The Art of Wall Street Investing involves two important primary principles. The first is to place one*s principal where it will be entirely secure, and the second to gain as large a percentage of return as possible without in the least disturbing or lessening the security of the principal. The moment the status of the principal is changed for the purpose of enhancing the rate of return, the transaction ceases to be a pure investment and becomes more or less of a speculation. Thus, analyzed in its simplest form, we may put it down as axiomatic that only those are legitimate investments where the primary motive is the safe securing of one's principal and the rate of return thereon is looked upon as secondary. A speculation, on the other

The Art of Wall Street Investing
By
John Moody

hand, is where the desire for large profit is so strong that the safety of the principal becomes in effect a minor consideration. That is to say, the person investing or speculating may regard his principal as secure but is willing to place it at considerable risk in order to increase his profit. The securing of the principal, therefore, is the first and chief matter to be considered in investing money.

Looked upon in this light, it will be seen that the matter of investing money wisely is a most important as well as a most difficult art, and therefore well worthy of careful examination. The ideas and suggestions embraced in the following pages are the concrete result of sixteen years* experience and study of Wall Street conditions and methods; and while it may appear to some that the writer is too conservative in his attitude towards investing methods in general, yet careful thought should convince every reader that it is the part of safety and prudence to be securely on the side of conservatism in Wall Street investing, rather than the reverse.

The Art of Wall Street Investing
By
John Moody

In the following chapters the general subject of Wall Street investing is treated in as practical a way as possible. The fundamental principles of investing are carefully examined, and their importance emphasized. It is in- tended that the book shall not be merely a treatise on the abstract or theoretical side of investing, nor that it shall merely give a surface view of the investment field. Rather is it intended to make the book of general use as a practical hand-book or guide for those who wish to place their money in legitimate corporate enterprises of the several kinds, through the purchase of stocks and bonds. Not only are the different classes of securities themselves described, but careful explanations are given of the machinery and methods of investing throughout the various Wall Street channels.

In the general arrangement and composition the valuable co-operation of Mr. John F. Hume, author of a book now long out of print, entitled "The Art of

The Art of Wall Street Investing
By
John Moody

Investing," is hereby publicly acknowledged.

JOHN MOODY 1906

The Art of Wall Street Investing
By
John Moody

CONTENTS

The Art of Wall Street Investing
By
John Moody

I
<u>Safety and Security</u>

UNLESS he has had much previous experience, the prospective investor who wishes to put his money at work through Wall Street channels, will be confronted at the outset with the questions of "safety" and "security." Knowing only more or less definitely, that he ought not to expect a return of more than four to five per cent., if he wishes to invest his money securely, he naturally seeks more expert advice from a banker, broker or general dealer in investment securities. And he is wise is doing this, provided he exercises good judgment in the selection of the broker or dealer. But brokers and dealers in investment securities are of course, not infallible; their judgment is sometimes biased, and they may, for one reason or another, give unsound advice. Hence it is all the more necessary that the investor should inform himself regarding the merits of a given security, as well as train himself in the art of analyzing investments in general.

The Art of Wall Street Investing
By
John Moody

The truth is, that while there are certain fixed rules for proper guidance, every bond must be judged by itself in order to be analyzed correctly. For instance, a man may be advised to invest only in "first mortgages," on the hypothesis that by putting this limitation upon his field of investment, he will thereby insure its safety. But such advice, applied broadly and without qualification, is essentially un- sound. A fourth, fifth or tenth mortgage on some properties may be far more secure than a first mortgage on others. For instance, the Reading Company 4s, selling at 104, are a much safer security than were the first mortgage bonds of the Centralia Chester RR, issued in 1895, although the former are an eighth mortgage on parts of the main-line of the Reading system and were originally a first mortgage on no part of the property. Yet they are well secured, while the other bond defaulted early in its life and its holders were obliged to sacrifice a large part of their principal in the reorganization which followed the

The Art of Wall Street Investing
By
John Moody

default. Thus it will be seen that to merely advise the investor to confine his investments to first mortgages may be most misleading.

Another unsafe method of judging the safety of bonds, is to assume that because they are secured on part of a large railroad system and "underlie" one or more issues of secondary bonds, their security is absolutely assured. This, like the former theory, contains some vital flaws, and while it holds good in the majority of instances, if followed in others, brings very disastrous results. Many large and important railroad corporations absorb tributary or competing lines under one plan or another, but they do not always guaranteed the securities of these lines.

Bond issues are frequently "assumed" by a controlling company, according to statements circulated, but unless they have been specifically guaranteed, either by the acquiring corporation or by some other equally responsible concern, it does not

The Art of Wall Street Investing
By
John Moody

necessarily follow that the credit of the latter is back of the security at all. The acquired line may turn out an unprofitable and losing investment, with the result that the larger or controlling line will want to either unload its burden or scale down the obligations of the branch to a sum approximately less than the latter is currently earning. There are many methods whereby this can be done, as has been proven many times. It is vital, therefore, that the investor should base his entire judgment of value on the property itself, regardless of the parent company, unless indeed the latter has absolutely assumed and guaranteed the principal and interest of the bond.

A third error, which is very common, is to assume that because a bond is listed on one or more of the stock exchanges, it is therefore safer or in better standing than otherwise. Such a notion is entirely unsound, as there are far more bonds of the highest grade and of the best security traded in on the various markets outside of the exchanges themselves. The chief

The Art of Wall Street Investing
By
John Moody

advantage of a security being listed on an exchange is that it thereby secures a fixed quotation, but the fact of its being listed does not bear upon its safety in any way. While it is true that many of the best secured bonds and stocks are listed on the exchanges, it is also true that many of the least secure are listed as well.

In contemplating an investment in a given security, each case should be judged on its own merits. In the case of a railroad bond, it is not the question of whether the issue is a first mortgage or a blanket mortgage, but whether the value of the property on which it is secured is sufficiently in excess of the amount of the mortgage, and whether the in- come from the property is sufficiently in excess of the amount required for meeting the interest on the bonds and all prior obligations. And in defining value, we mean, of course, permanent earning power, for it is chiefly the permanent or growing earning power that makes the value. For instance, the New York, New Haven and Hartford railroad lines, between New York and Boston, are

The Art of Wall Street Investing
By
John Moody

bonded and capitalized for an amount far in excess of the cost of replacing the actual movable property of the company. But there are other assets besides rails and equipment which make railroad property valuable. These are its location, its exclusive rights of way and terminal sites or privileges. It is from these that flow its chief earning power. The six hundred odd miles of railroad in the New Jersey Central system may not represent much more movable property than a like mileage of railroad in Mexico, and may not have originally cost much more to build. But the vast difference in value will be found in the location, in the value of the land, a value which has been created by the influx or growth of population. This is such an important factor that the value of a property at once appreciates if a tendency towards more rapid growth appears, while it tends to fall in all cases where the contrary tendency develops.

The rights of way and terminal sites and privileges are therefore the first features to bear in mind in analyzing the earning power, or value. And it must also

The Art of Wall Street Investing
By
John Moody

be borne in mind that it is the permanent, or average, earning power rather than the possible temporary income which is to be considered. By permanency is meant a matter of generations, rather than years. Most railroad bonds, nowadays, run from 40 to 100 years, and the investor must naturally be assured that there is not likely to be any real depreciation in the property, if properly maintained, in the generations to come. His first thought, then, must be to ascertain if the influx of population around and along the lines of the property promises to continue indefinitely; and at the same time he must determine whether the value of this and the surrounding land is such that the creation of a rival right of way is out of question.

*(This effect of population on land values is brought out most clearly and scientifically in a book recently written by Richard M. Hurd, President of the Mortgage Bond Co., New York, entitled "Principles of City Land Values."

The Art of Wall Street Investing
By
John Moody

In other words, his fundamental asset (the site) must be practically exclusive, for it is the condition of exclusiveness that gives it most of its value.

Having assured himself as to this, his next care will be to see that the probable average earning capacity of the property in the poorest times is well in excess (50 per cent, at least) of all requirements for interest on this mortgage and all prior charges, as well as for full maintenance of the property in every respect. The investigation of this phase of the enterprise is frequently a difficult one, as reports and income accounts are often so misleading in arrangement and make-up that the careless investor is frequently deceived by an elaborate display of figures which may mean very little. In Chapter IV, "Analyzing Railroad Securities," this subject of railroad accounting is referred to in full detail.

The Art of Wall Street Investing
By
John Moody

But even though the investor has thoroughly informed himself regarding the above characteristics, there are many other uncertainties which are to be avoided or overcome. However, if he has been careful to see that the conditions described above are all present in a given investment, his chances of losing his money will be reduced to a minimum. If, on the other hand, he neglects these precautions, and adopts other rules for analyzing the security or puts his trust in the "say-so" of this or that authority, then he stands in great danger of sooner or later coming to grief, as will be shown in the following pages.

Many years ago the careless legislation of many of the States permitted railroad and other corporations to decide for themselves, absolutely without restriction, the amounts of obligations they might put out, and therefore it was no wonder that the, privilege was abused, and the making of shares and bonds, the latter represented to be amply secured by mortgage liens,

The Art of Wall Street Investing
By
John Moody

were carried to criminal excess. One illustration will suffice.

The old Arkansas Central Railway company, located in the State of Arkansas, built only forty-eight miles of its projected road. The road was of narrow gauge, with very light iron, and in every way cheaply constructed. It cost less than ten thousand dollars per mile, including equipment. As has been the case with most companies building railways in new territory, help in its behalf was asked from the communities to be benefited, and their bonds, amounting to nearly half a million dollars, were given it by the counties, cities, etc. Under a Statute providing for aid to railroads when their beds could be utilized for levee purposes, the company got $160,000 of State bonds. Under another statute it got, as a loan from the State, the latter's bonds to the amount of $1,350,000, which were to be a first lien on the property. After such abundant assistance, it would have appeared hardly necessary for the company to put out obligations of its own.

The Art of Wall Street Investing
By
John Moody

However, it proceeded to market and issue its own debentures to the amount of $2,500,000, of which $1,200,000 purported to be secured by first mortgage, a representation that, for reasons already stated, was not correct. In addition, a considerable amount of stock certificates were issued. Altogether, nearly $5,000,000 of paper was put out and negotiated on the basis of forty-eight miles of narrow-gauge road. But this proved to be insufficient. The road, for non-payment of interest on its bonds, soon passed into the hands of a receiver, who found it in such an unfinished state, that with the court's permission, he issued a considerable amount of his own certificates to provide for necessary repairs and betterments. Then the road, the product of such an outlay, was sold at public auction and brought the magnificent sum of $40,000, which was paid, not in cash, but in receiver's certificates that had been purchased at a great discount from their face !

Twenty or thirty years ago, nearly all first class securities, outside of

The Art of Wall Street Investing
By
John Moody

"governments" and "municipals," were steam railroad bonds and stocks. But we now have stocks and bonds upon the market representing nearly all conceivable kinds of property, industrial and manufacturing companies, telegraphs, telephones, gas, electric light and traction companies, water-works, bridges oil and gas wells, factories and mills of every description, patent rights of all sorts, steamboat lines, apartment houses, realty enterprises, and even cemeteries. And not only are properties of many kinds used to issue bonds on, but many kinds of bonds are often issued upon the same properties. Thus we find among our railroads and other corporations not only first, second and third mortgages, but income bonds, debentures, convertible bonds, consolidated bonds, redemption bonds, renewal bonds, terminal bonds, divisional bonds, sinking fund bonds, "blanket-mortgage" bonds, collateral trust bonds, equipment bonds, participating bonds, joint bonds, and bonds ad nauseam until they lap and overlap in seemingly endless

The Art of Wall Street Investing
By
John Moody

complication. Not that merely, but one issue of bonds is sometimes made the basis of other issues. Indeed, one of the money-making devices of the time is the formation of companies that issue their bonds on the security of the other people's bonds that they have purchased, either yielding a higher rate of interest or obtained at lower prices than they expect to realize for their issues. There seems, in fact, to be no limit to the production of securities that are spread before capitalists and investors. There never was a time when it was so easy to invest money and to lose it. Of the securities that are offered with first rate recommendations it is probable that about one-third are actually good, one-third have some value, and one-third are practically worthless. Hence the very natural inference that whatever art there may be in the matter of investing is to be exercised chiefly in the avoidance of unworthy offerings, and it is to that point first that a profitable discussion must be mainly directed.

The Art of Wall Street Investing
By
John Moody

For the condition of things described, the laws of some of our States in giving corporations almost limitless power to issue negotiable paper, as well as in permitting all sorts of companies to incorporate themselves, are, undoubtedly, very largely to blame. Our banks are closely watched and very properly restrained from taking people's money on false pretenses ; but is it much better for industrial and other corporations to take it by means of legalized fictitious evidences of value? Banks and insurance companies are by no means the only institutions that need watching. One of the reforms that would seem to be worth consideration is legislation prohibitory of the creation by companies existing by authority of law of stocks and securities not representing cash actually paid into their treasuries, or proprietary interests whose values are to be determined by disinterested parties. Texas has incorporated substantially such a provision in her constitution. Her example should be followed by all other commonwealths.

The Art of Wall Street Investing
By
John Moody

But the security behind or beneath the debenture or other paper obligatory is not the only thing to be looked into by the investor. Even the form of the document may be import- ant. A case in point, inasmuch as it shows how the preparation of an undertaking for the payment of money may change its apparent value, would seem in this connection to be appropriately quoted. Some years ago certain townships in the State of Missouri were desirous of aiding the construction of railroads with their credit. The State Legislature, to that end. passed an act authorizing the issue and sale of bonds obligatory upon them ; but it was stipulated — a very singular provision — that, instead of being put out by the townships, the bonds should be executed by the officials of the counties in which they were located. Accordingly debentures aggregating several million dollars were thus prepared and disposed of. The bonds bore the seals of the counties and the signatures of their

The Art of Wall Street Investing
By
John Moody

officials. On the back and at the top of each signature, in large letters, were the words "county bond." The instrument began with the recital, in the usual form, that it was issued by the county, but farther on, and in the smallest type employed, came the statement that it was executed for and in behalf of a certain township, which alone was to be responsible for its payment. These bonds were extensively advertised as "county bonds," and probably in most instances, certainly in many, were sold as such, and it was not until purchasers parted with their money, that they discovered that, instead of getting the bonds of well-known and wealthy counties, they had secured only the obligations of townships they had never heard of before. It was then manifest enough that they had been made the victims of a piece of very sharp and very shabby practice. In many cases the buyers of bonds and other securities learn, when it is too late, that their purchases, owing to some obscure and apparently innocent passage that had been overlooked or disregarded, are very

The Art of Wall Street Investing
By
John Moody

different from what they thought they were getting. How often have careless investors that supposed they were purchasing undertakings that would be good for long terms of years, and probably paid premiums to obtain them, ascertained at the end of comparatively short intervals that they were forced to accept in payment the amounts nominated in the bonds in consequence of unnoticed clauses giving their makers power to redeem their option! The lesson of such cases is obvious enough. It is that no one should buy a bond or stock without first having carefully read the certificate. This may seem like an unnecessary warning ; but in truth it is a most material one. Thousands and thousands of dollars have been lost by the neglect of this simple precaution. "I didn't read the bond" is the explanation that has again and again been offered when time has disclosed a different investment from the one intended to be paid for. The fact is that comparatively few unprofessional bond and stock purchasers ever carefully examine the

The Art of Wall Street Investing
By
John Moody

instruments they acquire. They look at
the headings, those parts that are in big
letters, and take the rest for granted. It is
a most unwise practice. Unless you are
previously familiar with the document in
all its parts, don't fail to read it before
you buy. Read it all, the little the as well
as the big type, the indorsements, the
coupons, and all. Don't take somebody
else's word for it. Examine the seal, the
signatures, and even the embellishments.
Something may be disclosed that will
change your mind and save your money.

But if there are tricks in the making
of securities, even more are to be
apprehended in the selling of them, and
should be guarded against with
corresponding diligence. It is a notable
fact that no poor securities are ever
offered. They are always good so long as
they are on the market. It is only after
they have been purchased that they prove
to be worth- less. Interest has never been
known to fail on bonds that are seeking
investors, although default has
sometimes followed very closely on the

The Art of Wall Street Investing
By
John Moody

sale of the last obligations. Indeed, it is no secret that interest is sometimes paid out of the proceeds of the bonds, the purchasers in this way getting a portion of their own money back while the process of marketing them is going forward, although such a thing has seldom been known to happen after the entire issue has been disposed of. The advertisements of some bond-sellers are often marvelous productions. No such securities as they have to offer have ever been on the market before. They are absolutely safe; they pay extra rates of interest, etc., etc. The wonder is that with so much capital seeking investment, it is found necessary to advertise such perfections at all! In such cases it is hardly necessary to say that the only safe rule for investors is to find other uses for their money, however strong the temptation may be.

A common expedient of bond-makers and bond-merchants is to fortify their issues with the favorable opinions of eminent lawyers. This is particularly the case when the obligations of

The Art of Wall Street Investing
By
John Moody

municipalities or of companies that are dependent upon contracts with municipalities are offered, some municipalities having in the past shown an unpleasant disposition to go back on their undertakings. No exceptions can be taken to the practice referred to, as counsel learned in the law should in such cases always be consulted; but the writer has to say that he has never yet known a security so poor that a lawyer's opinion could not be had to back it. Such testimonials should be taken for what they are worth, and no more.

When so many seductive baits are offered; so many nets and traps, contrived and constructed by clever brains and cunning fingers, are spread for the capture of those having money, is it surprising that the careless and credulous are victimized, and even that the sagacious and prudent should sometimes be taken in? Nevertheless, for the losses they have sustained, investors, as a rule, have themselves chiefly to blame. The mistakes made, in nine cases out of ten, have been the purchase of

The Art of Wall Street Investing
By
John Moody

"cheap" securities. The hope of realizing a little more than ordinary interest, by buying paper at a discount, has proved to be the rock on which unnumbered capitalists have split. In addition to their money's worth, they have endeavored to get something for nothing, with the result of most generally getting nothing for something. It is remarkable how blind are people, ordinarily sagacious enough to make money, to the fact that property cannot pay a revenue beyond its producing capacity. For instance, how can a trolley company, whose line is wholly or mainly built from the proceeds of mortgage bonds, sell them at a heavy discount, besides allowing large commissions for the selling, and then pay both this interest and dividends on a large issue of watered stock? Or how can a poor agriculturist, occupying a half-improved farm out on the frontier, with a family to support and grain selling barely above the cost of production, pay ten or twelve per cent, upon the capital with which he does business?

The Art of Wall Street Investing
By
John Moody

By what rule or rules is the investor to govern himself. No formula can guarantee him absolute safety. One thing, however, he can properly count upon, viz., that he must expect to pay a fair price for a good security—one that will return him no more than a moderate interest on his money. If he wants to speculate and is willing to take risks, that is another thing. He can then look for bargains. The capitalist or investor who sends his money into a new section, or puts it into a new mechanical process, or a new constructive enterprise, may or may not make a hit, but for the ordinary and conservative operator, the conditions of the commercial and financial world give warning that only reasonable profits are to be looked for. The first and main thing to be studied is safety. And yet there is such a thing as going too far in the matter of prudence. The investor may pay too dearly for safety. There are securities which, compared with others that are to be had, sell at prices much above their real worth. The reason is that everybody knows them to be good, and

The Art of Wall Street Investing
By
John Moody

investors who don't want to take the trouble to investigate, or are afraid to trust both their own judgment and the counsels of their friends, are willing to pay extra prices for them. But there are plenty of others that may be had at lower figures, which are just as good. There is no reason in the world why the investor should not safely invest at a rate that will generally yield him 4 per cent, to 5 per cent, interest, and have his investment as secure as any property can be under human supervision. As heretofore stated, with the creation of new enterprises and properties, and the development of old ones, new securities are constantly appearing in this country and a fair share of them ought to be good. Indeed, our securities ought to be the best in the world. The sure and rapid growth of our resources supplies a reliable support as long as fair intelligence and common honesty attend their production. The only thing is to choose with discretion, so many doubtful and even fraudulent issues appearing at the same time; but

The Art of Wall Street Investing
By
John Moody

no more judgment is really demanded than in purchasing lands or cattle.

Two common and often fatal mistakes should be avoided. One is in relying solely upon the advice of another. No one competent to form an opinion for himself should put his pecuniary interests unreservedly in the keeping of another. Such absolute confidence invites betrayal. By far the greater number of losses to investors have been in securities purchased exclusively on the recommendation of interested outside parties. While it is well to get the opinion of a reputable broker, the purchaser should investigate for himself. The other mistake is to uniformly give preference to listed securities. As pointed out at the beginning of this article, many persons seem to think that stocks and bonds must have a value if they are quoted at some stock exchange, forgetting how many fancies have been ballooned until they have burst at such places. On the contrary, such a position is likely to expose them to manipulation for purely speculative purposes. Stock-exchange

The Art of Wall Street Investing
By
John Moody

quotations are often unsafe guides to buyers. They represent not merely the value of the property but also the pitch of speculation at the time. When securities are converted into foot-balls for gamblers to play with, they are pretty certain to be too high or too low. The main advantage they can have is a readier marketability in case of an urgent need to sell ; but it is at the times when such need is likely to exist that they are pretty certain to be at the lower point. No speculative help can long take the place of real value. Securities, in the long run, must stand upon their merits, and purchasers have merely to follow business principles as taught by the canons of common sense.

In seeking investments, and especially long time investments^ there are several things to be taken into account. There is not only the question of the kind of security to purchase, but the question of the time of purchase. There are opportunities to be looked for as well as pitfalls to be shunned. It is during periods and seasons of depression, when securities are forced upon the market,

The Art of Wall Street Investing
By
John Moody

often to be sacrificed — and such opportunities are certain to come if waited for long enough — that the shrewd investor finds his richest harvest. That, however, cannot be said of the ordinary investor. He usually buys when securities are up and confidence is unimpaired, and becoming frightened as the market values go down, sells when they are at the bottom, and holds his money to reinvest in something else no better, and probably not as good, when the tide has turned. As a rule, the best time to invest is when others are unloading. In money matters it is never safe to follow "the crowd." Nor is it safe, (which is little more than the expression of the same idea in another form) to purchase a security when it is on the "boom." A peculiarity of our money market, conservative as it is popularly supposed to be, is that it is constantly changing its favorites. Its offerings come in waves. Its dealings at one time may be chiefly in railways, at another in industrial obligations, and at another the excitement may run to mining shares or mortgages on ranches and real estate.

The Art of Wall Street Investing
By
John Moody

For the time all professional brokers and bond and share sellers urge their customers to adopt the popular issue, of which, as the result of the increased demand, there is almost certain to be excessive, if not fraudulent production. To yield to the pressure of such a time is always risky. Old and tried securities, like old friends, are likely to be the truest and best.

One thing the investor would do well never to forget, is that there are always plenty of good securities in the market. No one with money need ever fear that others will get all the solid investments, and, in the apprehension that there will not be enough of that sort to go around, put up with an inferior article. Don't let him choose what is not altogether satisfactory, under the impression that nothing else as good or better will offer. If he does so, sooner or later he will regret it. Something good always comes to him who waits with money in his hand.

Another thing of a precautionary nature it is well enough for the investor to do, and that is to scatter his purchases.

The Art of Wall Street Investing
By
John Moody

The old adage about not putting all the eggs in one basket applies with peculiar force to investments. The tendency with those having moderate sums to invest, and who need to be the most circumspect, is to make up their minds in favor of a single line of securities and put everything there. Of course, a failure in that quarter is particularly disastrous. The writer knew a man, some years ago, who decided in favor of municipal obligations, saying that he had satisfied himself that, on the whole, there was nothing else so reliable. Accordingly he put his entire available means into them. But practicing abundant precaution, as he supposed, he divided his money equally among municipal issues of Illinois, Missouri and Kansas, they having the most paper at that time on the market. He thought he was entirely safe as to principal. But soon after a wave of repudiation sentiment swept over that part of the country, and every one of his bonds were left in default. It is well enough to scatter in kind as well as in locality.

The Art of Wall Street Investing
By
John Moody

Against the theory of scattering investments, men sometimes quote the advice of **Andrew Carnegie to "put all your eggs in one basket, and watch the basket."** This principle, however, while sound enough for the expert or specialist who is in a situation to at all times see and watch the basket, is not applicable to the average ordinary investor. The average investor simply cannot "watch the basket" in the way implied by **Mr. Carnegie**, and therefore it is a safe principle for him under all ordinary circumstances, to limit his chances of loss to the greatest possible extent through a wide and judicious distribution of his capital.

The Art of Wall Street Investing
By
John Moody

II

Bonds and what they represent

BONDS are issued on all kinds of property and are usually secured by a mortgage of some kind. There are, however, certain classes of bonds, such as "governments" and "municipals," the principal of which is secured entirely in other ways. It will be of interest and profit to briefly point out the earmarks of these different classes of bonds.

Bonds are usually issued in denominations of $1,000 each, though sometimes issued for a larger or smaller amount. Some bonds bear coupons and some are what are known as registered bonds. The interest on the latter is always paid directly to the registered owner by

The Art of Wall Street Investing
By
John Moody

check, in the same manner that dividends are paid.

A first mortgage bond is always secured by a deed of trust, and directly covers the property on which it is secured without being subject to any other lien. There may be other bond issues secured on the same property, but their lien is entirely subsequent to the first mortgage. Because a bond is a "first mortgage" one should not necessarily assume that it is a "gilt-edged" security. True, it is bound to be better than any other bonds secured on the same property, but the property itself may not be worth the amount of the mortgage, or the business may not be earning enough to pay the interest as it falls due.

A second mortgage bond, is, as its name indicates, always secured subsidiary to the prior, or first mortgage. If the first mortgage completely covers the value of the property, then of course, the second mortgage has an inferior standing only. But many first mortgages amount to only a portion of the value of a property, and in these cases a second mortgage is

The Art of Wall Street Investing
By
John Moody

frequently well secured and attractive as an investment. To illustrate: A property worth $10,000,000 and earning $800,000 per year may have issued a first mortgage amounting to $1,000,000, and carrying an interest charge of $60,000 per year. Such a first mortgage bond would be regarded as high grade. The company may then have issued a second mortgage amounting to $2,000,000, and carrying an interest charge of $120,000 per annum. In this case the second mortgage bond would be high grade also, as the aggregate amount of both mortgages would be but $3,000,000 on a property valued at $10,000,000, and the total interest charge of $180,000 would leave a surplus, (based on earnings of $800,000 per year) aggregating $620,000, or more than 3.5 times the interest charge itself. On the other hand, if a property, the value of which was but $4,000,000, with annual earnings of but $240,000, should issue first and second mortgages of the character and amounts mentioned above, not only would the second mortgage bond be of doubtful quality, but the first

The Art of Wall Street Investing
By
John Moody

mortgage itself would be regarded as very far from "high-grade."

Third, fourth and fifth mortgages, etc., are, as their names indicate, secured subsequent to the several preceding issues and require no separate comment, except that the mere fact of their being subsidiary to several issues does not of itself make them inferior in value. Other things being equal, the title of a bond signifies very little. The fifth mortgage bond of the old New York Erie Railroad (now assumed by the Erie Railroad system) and of which there are outstanding $700,000, are not any the less valuable because they are secured as a "fifth" mortgage only, but on the other hand they are decidedly high-grade in respect to security, as they are a lien (subject to four prior mortgages aggregating $13,500,000) on 446 miles of the Erie main lines. As these main lines are easily worth ten times the amount of all five mortgages, it will be seen at a glance that they are all securities of a most desirable kind.

The Art of Wall Street Investing
By
John Moody

A consolidated mortgage bond is generally created as a result of a reorganization, a readjustment of finances, or for the purpose of providing new capital where a property is already mortgaged to some extent, and a second or third mortgage would not be well enough secured to warrant a ready sale. To cite an instance, let us take the First Consolidated 5% bonds of the Southern Railway Company. This Company was formed in 1894 as successor to a large number of other railroad corporations operating throughout the South. It was necessary to finance the new company with liberal capital, to spend a large amount of money on the properties, and in these and other ways to increase the earning power of the company. As the properties were already mortgaged in various ways for more than $60,000,000, it was not found practicable for the company to issue an independent mortgage. They therefore authorized a "consolidated" mortgage, one of the cardinal features being the authorization of a very large issue, of which a sufficient

The Art of Wall Street Investing
By
John Moody

amount were held in reserve to retire the various prior divisional mortgages as they matured. This consolidated issue runs 100 years, and as the many divisional and prior bonds mature at different dates and some very quickly, it follows that the "consolidated" bonds grow in security and value as the old issues are cancelled. In this particular case every prior issue will be retired by 1938 and most of them much sooner, whereupon the consolidated issue will become a first mortgage.

A general mortgage bond is of the same class as a consolidated mortgage. This is sometimes called a "blanket" mortgage, and is frequently issued when there is but a single first mortgage on the property. It is sometimes partly secured by second mortgage and partly by first mortgage, but usually it is merely subsequent to two or more first and sometimes even consolidated or less well secured liens. When this is the case a sufficient amount is generally reserved to take care of the other bonds as they mature. In some cases the prior liens, or

The Art of Wall Street Investing
By
John Moody

portions of them, are exchanged for the "generals" on a mutually satisfactory basis.

A prior lien bond is not necessarily a bond of prior security at all, except in a qualified sense. The term "prior lien" as applied to railroad bonds nowadays, connotes something entirely different from what would naturally be supposed. The Erie Railroad "prior lien" fours, for instance, are simply prior to the "general lien" fours, and both are part of an issue of a first consolidated mortgage which was authorized at the time of the reorganization in 1895 to provide new capital, take care of old mortgages, etc. The prior lien issue, therefore, simply has preference over the general lien portion of the same mortgage. The Northern Pacific, Baltimore and Ohio, and a number of other large railroad companies have adopted a similar device.

A debenture bond is not a mortgage, but simply a promissory note, or promise to pay. It is usually issued in the same form as other bonds, sometimes carrying coupons and sometimes appearing in

The Art of Wall Street Investing
By
John Moody

registered form. While both principal and interest are an obligation of the company issuing the bond, yet in the case of a default the holder cannot foreclose as he can in the case of a mortgage bond. In this respect the debenture is in very much the same position as a cumulative preferred stock, with the important exception that the latter usually carries a voting power, while the former does not. But debenture bonds, like all the rest, get their investment status largely through the character of the corporation issuing them. Some debenture issues, like those on the Chicago ; Northwestern system, are in such high standing (because of the vastness and general solidity of the company) as to be quoted at a very high premium, the fives selling at over 115 — while others are in the category of third-rate stocks.

A collateral trust bond is an indirect mortgage on a piece of property, made through the deposit with a trustee of other securities which are usually directly secured. Sometimes, how- ever, the collateral so deposited consists of both

The Art of Wall Street Investing
By
John Moody

stocks and bonds, and in some cases, of stocks only. Like other kinds of bonds, there are "all sorts and conditions" of collateral issues, some being secured by one collateral only and others being secured by a heterogeneous variety of good, bad and indifferent stocks and bonds. In some cases bonds are secured partly by deposit of collateral and partly by mortgage on some property. In such instances they are described as "mortgagecollateral trust bonds," etc.

A convertible bond is an issue which carries a right or privilege for conversion into some other issue of bonds or stocks. There are many kinds of convertible bonds, and they carry convertible clauses for many and diverse reasons. Thus, United States Steel Corporation second fives were convertible into preferred stock at par; Erie Railroad four per cent, convertibles are convertible into common stock on the basis of $200 in stock for $100 in Bonds before April 1, 1915; Baltimore; Ohio convertible debentures are convertible into common stock at par on any interest day, etc.

The Art of Wall Street Investing
By
John Moody

Sometimes these clauses are inserted in mortgages to give them a speculative value; in other cases to provide for the retirement of the debt by its conversion into stock. Usually the act of converting is optional with the holder.

A joint bond is one issued or assumed by two or more corporations. Thus, the Great Northern-Northern Pacific joint collateral trust fours, secured by deposit of Chicago, Burlington; Quincy Railroad stock are the joint obligation of the two controlling companies.

There are not a great many issues of such joint-bonds, although there are many cases where independent bond issues are jointly guaranteed, either by two or more separate corporations.

A guaranteed bond is one the payment of which is specifically "guaranteed" by endorsement or otherwise by another corporation. There are many guaranteed bond issues in the railroad field, carrying guarantees of various kinds. In some cases the interest only is guaranteed; in others, both the

The Art of Wall Street Investing
By
John Moody

principal and interest. Guarantees often
come about as the result of a
consolidation, lease or absorption of some
kind, although there are many cases in
which bonds are guaranteed for other
reasons. The Delaware, Lackawanna ;
Western Railway specifically guarantees
the Morris; Essex refunding 3.5% bonds.
But the Morris; Essex is a constituent
part of the Delaware, Lackawanna;
Western system, and the bonds would be
equally as valuable without the guarantee
as they are with it. The guarantee,
however, makes them a direct obligation
of the Delaware, Lackawanna ; Western
Railway. There are many guaranteed
issues, which are, of course, materially
improved by their guarantee, and which
without it would not only be unattractive,
but would be entirely unsalable, for the
reason that the property on which they
are directly secured is not valuable
enough in itself or has not the necessary
earning power. It must not be assumed,
however, that the mere formal guarantee
gives the bond its value. This latter
depends entirely upon the standing and

The Art of Wall Street Investing
By
John Moody

financial strength of the guarantor. Thus, a bond issue guaranteed by the New York Central system will have a far better standing than one guaranteed by a company like the Denver ; Southwestern, the standing of which has been of a more or less uncertain and speculative nature.

Investors in guaranteed bonds should examine their security very closely to ascertain whether the guarantee can be abrogated in any way, and whether it actually covers both principal and interest. If the guaranteeing company itself seems likely to ever repudiate the bond, its entire value will then, of course, revert back to the standing of the mortgage itself, and in any event, this latter should be investigated with care. The guarantee of a bond is usually embraced in the phraseology of the bond itself, or else is specifically stated by the actual endorsement of the guarantor.

An assumed bond is in some respects similar to a guaranteed bond, being an issue, the payment of which, both principal and interest, is "assumed"

The Art of Wall Street Investing
By
John Moody

by the controlling company. The effect is in some sense the same as a guarantee and the bond becomes, as a result, a direct obligation of the assuming corporation. There are many hundreds of "assumed" bonds dealt on Wall Street, of every kind and description. Great care should be taken, however, in examining a so-called assumed bond. Many large railroad corporations have acquired control of other properties without actually assuming their obligations. Frequently the acquiring company, for strategic or other reasons, voluntarily takes care of these obligations, without being legally obligated to do so. But unless a bond issue has been definitely and formally assumed by the controlling company, its standing as an investment must depend chiefly on the actual property itself and not on the standing of the controlling corporation. Instances of assumed bonds are such as the Kentucky Central; Atlantic, Knoxville ; Northern and the Evansville, Henderson ; Nashville issues in the Louisville ; Nashville system. The payment of both principal

The Art of Wall Street Investing
By
John Moody

and interest of these issues has been made an obligation of the controlling company. On the same system we find several mortgages of the Nashville, Chattanooga; St. Louis Railway which have not been "assumed" at all. These issues stand entirely on their own merits, and are an obligation of the Nashville, Chattanooga; St. Louis Railway only, the latter being controlled through stock ownership, by the Louisville; Nashville Railroad.

A divisional bond is usually an obligation of a large railroad which is secured on some specific division of the property. On the Chicago, Milwaukee ; St. Paul Railway all the bond issues, outside of the general mortgage, are divisional liens. Thus, the Iowa; Dakota Division 7s are a direct obligation, but secured by mortgage on the division extending from Algoma, Iowa, to Chamberlain, South Dakota, consisting of 355 miles. The Chicago; Lake Superior Division first 5s are a direct obligation, but secured by direct mortgage on 75 miles of road extending from Rockland, Illinois, to

The Art of Wall Street Investing
By
John Moody

Portage City, Michigan. The cardinal distinction between a divisional and an assumed bond is that the former is a direct obligation and is usually issued by the main corporation, while the latter is (or originally was) the obligation of a subsidiary corporation, the ownership or control of the stock or property of which has been acquired, or is possessed by the main company. Assumed bonds are sometimes spoken of as divisional issues, and in a broad sense they are, but the specific meaning of the term is as explained above.

An income bond is one on which the payment of the interest is dependent on income. That is to say, while the principal is a mortgage and legally must be taken care of at maturity, the interest rate is not a "fixed charge," and no foreclosure proceedings can be instituted in case the interest is not paid. The payment of the latter is entirely dependent on the earnings of the company, it being generally agreed that if the interest is earned it shall be paid; otherwise, not. There are several classes of income

The Art of Wall Street Investing
By
John Moody

bonds. Some are not a mortgage. These are usually known as "debenture incomes." Others bear a cumulative clause which provides that interest when unpaid, shall accrue, and all accrued interest be paid or satisfied before the current interest is paid. These are known as cumulative income bonds. Still others are convertible into securities of another class, such as preferred stock, and are known as convertible incomes. Others have preference over inferior issues and are known as preference incomes. Thus on the Central of Georgia Railway there are issues of first, second and third incomes, all carrying the right to 5% interest per annum, when earned. In this instance 5% must be paid on the firsts before the seconds receive anything, and the seconds must of course receive their 5% before the thirds come in for any interest. If enough is earned to pay the full amount on the firsts, but not enough for the full amount on the seconds, then the latter usually receive what- ever amount of the divisible income is left. This may amount to 1% or 3%% or 4%,

The Art of Wall Street Investing
By
John Moody

being dependent on what the road may be currently earning.

It does not follow, however, that interest is always paid on income bonds, even when the property earns it. One frequently hears the remark, that such and such a company is "showing" the full interest on its incomes or the full dividend on its preferred shares. "Showing" is not necessarily paying, and payments depend not merely on the earnings, but also on the judgment of the management as to whether it is wise to make the payments. Some managements are far more conservative in this respect than others, and the most far-seeing and cautious men, who handle the finances of a large property, will generally "go slow" in the matter of paying out money on incomes and dividends unless the company is earning a considerable surplus over the amount required for the payment, or has already accumulated a tangible surplus from earnings to fall back upon.

A sinking-fund mortgage is one which carries a provision setting aside a

The Art of Wall Street Investing
By
John Moody

portion of earnings year by year for the purpose of retiring the bonds at or before maturity. There are many kinds of sinking-fund clauses in bonds and they act in several different ways. The best known form is a provision requiring the company to deposit with the trustee periodically a certain sum of money, sometimes a percentage of the gross or net earnings, sometimes a percentage of the outstanding issue, and sometimes simply a fixed sum of money each year ; the trustee then either calling in by lot a sufficient number of the issue to exhaust the amount of money he has received, or, if more are offered at the callable price (this price is usually a premium figure, 102, 105, no, etc.), then buying the bonds in the open market at the lowest prices offered. The bonds so acquired are then cancelled and thus the issue is gradually reduced. Other forms of sinking funds are where the bonds so acquired by the trustee are "kept alive," the interest which is paid thereon being added to the fund and used for the purpose of buying still more bonds. Still other funds require

The Art of Wall Street Investing
By
John Moody

that the bond issue itself be allowed to run until maturity and that the money set aside in the fund be invested in other securities, and thus the whole fund is held intact until the entire bond issue actually matures.

There are a great many "sinking-fund" bonds in existence, but in the railroad investment field, they are not as popular nowadays as in former times. The permanent investor does not like a sinking-fund which may result in disturbing his investment at any time, even if he does receive a little premium, and this is especially true of savings banks and large corporate investors like insurance companies, large estates, etc. Furthermore, in the case of a bond which is subject to call, an artificial value is created; it will not sell much above the callable price, for the reason that it is callable at any time. On the other hand, if there is but little market for the bonds an artificial demand is created at the time of each sinking-fund purchase, and thus its attractions as an investment purchase are seriously interfered with. In the

The Art of Wall Street Investing
By
John Moody

matter of municipal securities, however, the sinking-fund is far more logical and useful, and particularly is it necessary in bonds which are issued for the construction of public utilities such as water, electric light and gas plants, which (where owned by municipalities) are operated at approximate cost and are not supposed to set aside surplus earnings in other ways to cover depreciation, expansions and improvements. This is also true of the more speculative classes of bonds, such as those on public service corporations in private hands, industrial enterprises, etc. Such cannot, as a rule, have too much safe-guarding of this nature. Railway industries of all kinds which have not had the opportunity of demonstrating their permanency or soundness over long periods of time should always carry sinking-funds in their bond issues. This is particularly applicable to industrial enterprises, the property of which constantly tends to depreciate. The great United States Steel Corporation carries many kinds of sinking-funds, aggregating in total

The Art of Wall Street Investing
By
John Moody

amount nearly $35,000,000 per annum, which at the present time is equal to more than 20% of the annual net income of all the plants. Bonds on coal mines and other mining properties also usually carry sinking-funds. In the case of the former the proviso usually is that a certain amount (often 2 or 3 cents) be set aside with every ton of coal mined, the accumulations being used in the usual ways for the retirement periodically of the issue.

An extended bond is an issue which has matured and by agreement with the owners has been extended for a further period, instead of a new issue being created to take its place. Often bonds are extended for a few years only, but sometimes the extension reaches on over several decades. Usually, in the case of railroad issues, the rate of interest is reduced at the time of the extension and sometimes new bonds of the same mortgage, but with sheets of coupons at reduced rates, are exchanged for the old ones. There have been instances where the old bonds have been retained and

The Art of Wall Street Investing
By
John Moody

stamped with the "extension clause," and new sheets of coupons supplied separately.

There are several issues of extended bonds now running as divisional liens on the Erie Railroad system. These are the New York; Erie first, second, third, fourth and fifth mortgages. Originally issued in the '40s and '50s at 7%, they all matured in the '70s and '80s, and have been extended for forty to fifty years more at 4, 4.5 and 5%. When they finally mature again they will this time be retired, and bonds of the Erie Railroad general lien issue, now held in reserve, will take their places.

An underlying bond is a general term describing any issue which precedes or is prior in mortgage security to some subsequent issue. When a bond is spoken of as underlying, it is generally so referred to in connection with some general or junior issue, which may or may not provide for retiring this issue at maturity. Thus any bond issue is "underlying" which has a junior security following it. Hence, a bond need not

The Art of Wall Street Investing
By
John Moody

necessarily be a first mortgage to be described as "underlying." It may itself be subject to a further mortgage or mortgages which underlie it. On many railroad systems, and indeed in other corporations there are frequently several "layers" of underlying issues, and on portions of the Erie and of the Reading systems, there are as many as ten mortgages secured, "underlying," or, if you wish to reverse the viewpoint, "overlying" one another.

A refunding mortgage bond is an issue especially created for taking care of maturing issues, supplying additional capital, etc., and for reducing fixed charges. The modern refunding bond on steam railroads is usually an issue running one hundred years, bearing a comparatively low rate of interest, and generally secured by a "blanket" mortgage on "all the property now owned or hereafter acquired," subject, of course, to the prior mortgages which are to be retired as they fall due. Often, a very large issue is authorized, in order that funds may be available for future

The Art of Wall Street Investing
By
John Moody

acquisitions. One of the first large refunding issues was that of the New York Central 3.5% refunding mortgage issued in June, 1897. The authorized issue was $100,000,000, of which $70,397,333 were originally reserved to retire certain prior liens, with $14,622,667 for premiums on the bonds. The remaining $15,000,000 were to be issued for new construction or property, after Dec. 31, 1903, at a rate not exceeding $1,000,000 per annum.

In authorizing these bonds the maturity of several underlying liens was anticipated by a few years. It so appened that all the mainline mortgages on the New York Central sys- tem matured between 1897 and 1905, and in authorizing the new 3%% mortgage it was made a part of the plan to allow holders to exchange their old bonds at once, on an equitable basis, and without waiting for the dates of maturity. This exchange plan was made optional with the old bondholders, but a large proportion of them took advantage of it. Today all the prior liens have been retired and nearly

The Art of Wall Street Investing
By
John Moody

$85,000,000 of the three and one-half per cents are today outstanding. It will be observed that they are now an actual first lien on the main lines of the system, and their refunding features have ceased to be a factor. There are today a large number of refunding issues, and because of their improving position, the length of time they run, and so forth, they are generally more popular with permanent investors than the prior issues which usually underlie them.

A participating bond is a modern term describing an issue which is entitled to participate in income or profits, under certain conditions, beyond its fixed rate of interest. The most notable instance of a participating bond were the Oregon Short Line Railroad participating fours, issued in 1902, but called for payment and cancelled on February 1, 1905. These bonds were issued to finance the purchase by the Union Pacific interests of Northern Securities Company stock, and the latter was deposited as collateral with the trustee. The mortgage required that in addition to receiving 4% interest, the

The Art of Wall Street Investing
By
John Moody

bonds were to participate in any dividends over 4% that the Northern Securities Company stock might pay. Thus, when the Northern Securities Company dividend rate was increased to 5%, these bonds received a dividend of 1% in addition to their regular interest, and of course shared, to an extent, in the speculative value thus engendered by an additional division of profits. The Northern Securities merger being afterward set aside, these participating bonds were largely converted into a new refunding issue of fours, guaranteed by the Union Pacific Railroad, and the balance were called and paid off at the redemption price of one hundred and five.

An equipment bond is an issue created to acquire equipment, and is secured directly upon locomotives, cars, and so forth. It frequently happens that a railroad finds it necessary to increase its equipment rapidly in order to handle a growing business in the most economical way. In most cases, large purchases of this kind involve the borrowing of money, as railroads do not always have funds

The Art of Wall Street Investing
By
John Moody

available for such purposes. In view of this situation, "equipment trusts" or equipment bonds have been invented. These usually run for short periods only, generally being paid off in installments or serially, ranging over several years. In some cases the payment of the principal of these equipment mortgages is done out of current earnings; in other cases out of the proceeds of other bond issues. Often there are several issues of equipment obligations on large properties, maturing at different periods and secured on different groups of locomotives and cars. Equipment bonds usually bear the current rates of interest which may be prevailing for a good security at the time they are issued. They are nearly always a well-protected obligation, as they cover tangible property, the value of which is easily determined.

In addition to the foregoing, there are various other designations sometimes given to bond issues, such as land grant bonds, trust mortgage bonds, currency bonds, and so forth, which have either been covered in the more general terms

The Art of Wall Street Investing
By
John Moody

described in the foregoing pages, or else carry names which are sufficient descriptions in themselves. Thus, currency bonds are issues which bear no "gold clause," but are payable, principal and interest, in the currency of the country, whatever that may happen to be. During the days of the free-silver agitation, and for nearly a decade before, nearly all railroads and financiers inserted the "gold clause" in bonds, which was simply a statement printed in full on each bond and coupon to the effect that the issue would be paid, not in "money" or "currency," but in gold. Thus, the gold clause came to be a feature of the utmost importance, for it was almost universally held (and especially in Wall Street) that free coinage of silver would mean an appreciation of one hundred per cent, in the value of gold as measured by the money standard. Whether this would have occurred or not is still a mooted question among the students of the currency problem, but in reality, if the railroads had, under such a condition, been obliged to pay in gold, it will be seen

The Art of Wall Street Investing
By
John Moody

that they would all have defaulted on both principal and interest. Therefore the "gold clause" was largely sentimental after all. Like the guarantee clause of a bond whose guarantor had not the proper resources to take care of its obligations in case the demand came upon him, so the gold clause, while sentimentally beneficial to sellers of bonds, could not have been of much practical usefulness if the actual conditions had come about which it was created to circumvent. But, as in every other walk of life, *unsound premises are often cherished and erected into superstitions in Wall Street*, and there are many eminent men there to this day, who will still hotly contest that it is just as necessary as ever to put the "gold clause" in a bond, to avoid all danger of depreciation; in spite of the fact that gold is now tending to depreciate and holding down the prices of bonds as a result.

The chief point to be emphasized in the chapter on **Bonds and What They Represent** is that the mere title of an issue may mean nothing from the standpoint of safety and value. These

The Art of Wall Street Investing
By
John Moody

descriptive details refer in no way to the value of a specific bond, but simply to the anatomy of the different issues.
Invariably the rule should be, when selecting a bond for investment, whether it is a direct mortgage, a consolidated or a general issue, a collateral trust or an income, a debenture or a refunding bond, to learn something of the property which it represents. If it is a railroad, what its capital is and what its earnings are, who its managers or controlling interests are; its alliances and rivalries; its territory and its strategic position; its past history and future prospects. These are general fundamental matters of the first importance, and it is through neglect of such knowledge that a large proportion of investors are misled or go astray. As an example, let me cite the ease of the Rock Island Company. This is a very large corporation, with capital running into the hundreds of millions and controlling in the neighborhood of 18,000 miles of railway lines. Its securities are about as heterogeneous as they could possibly be made, even if they had been created and

The Art of Wall Street Investing
By
John Moody

brought together by design rather than by accident. In all there are upwards of seventy bond issues on the system, including nearly every conceivable kind of mortgage, good, doubtful and indifferent. There are first mortgages of very inferior worth and bonds not mortgages at all, and yet of high standing. How easy it is, therefore, to err in passing upon bonds in this system, unless a good deal of general fundamental knowledge is first acquired. Thus one might naturally assume that the four per cent, collateral bonds of this company, due in 2002, were a sounder investment than the refunding fours of 1934, or that the gold fours of 1908-18 were better secured than the general mortgage fours of 1988. A little expert knowledge in these matters will set the judgment right, however ; and this fundamental knowledge once gained and uniformly employed in the judging of bonds will always prove of infinite value to the prospective investor in Wall Street.

The Art of Wall Street Investing
By
John Moody

III

Stocks and What they Are

THE cardinal distinction between bonds and stocks is clear, simple and concisely explained. Bonds represent or are secured by liens on property. Stocks are the property. Sometimes people fail to realize that stocks are the property itself and persist in assuming that they are merely a sort of legal attachment to it. But this is entirely erroneous. When one owns stock in the United States Steel Corporation, he is actually a part owner of those great properties, but if he owns a bond of this corporation he merely shares with others a mortgage which is secured on the property. Hence, if a stockholder, he gains or loses when the property appreciates or depreciates in earning power or value; but if a bond holder in a well-secured mortgage, he neither gains nor loses as the earnings and business

The Art of Wall Street Investing
By
John Moody

rises or falls, but his asset remains practically stationary in value. Stocks are also affected by various other influences which in no way affect bonds. Thus, the stockholder, being a joint owner with others of the actual property, therefore has, at least theoretically, a voice in its management. This "voice" is represented in his voting power, each stockholder having the right to cast one vote for each share of stock he owns, at annual meetings called together for the election of officers and directors, or at special meetings called for various other purposes, such as authorizing mortgages, new issues of stock, etc., etc. Usually preferred and common stocks have equal voting power, but there are exceptions where this is not true, and where the preferred shares have two or more votes to the common stockholders one. On the other hand cases exist where the preferred stockholders waive their voting power in consideration of receiving regularly a specified rate of dividends, and only re-assume their right in case their income is discontinued. This same

The Art of Wall Street Investing
By
John Moody

provision has sometimes been made in bond issues, usually income or debenture bonds.

A common stock is an issue which bears the designation "common" to distinguish it from a "preferred" issue of the same corporation. If no preferred issue exists, the qualifying word "common" is not necessary and is not usually employed. In such cases the issue is simply referred to as such and such a stock. Many of the railroads and industrials which are dealt in in Wall Street have both common and preferred issues, however. Roads like the New York Central, Pennsylvania, etc., are the exception rather than the rule. Of one hundred and thirty-four railroads and industrials whose issues are "active" on the Stock Exchange and are daily quoted in papers like the New York Evening Post, eighty-eight have both preferred and common stocks outstanding, while only forty-six have but one class of stock.

Common stock is generally entitled to dividends from earnings only after all prior charges and preferred stock

The Art of Wall Street Investing
By
John Moody

dividends have been satisfied. In other words, it is the last security to be taken care of in the dividing of profits. Hence, the common stock is more often a speculative or semi-speculative security than preferred stocks or bonds. In many cases common stocks have never received dividends and probably never will. Their chief value, under such conditions, is measured partly by their voting power and partly by the fluctuating value of the equity in the property of which they are shares. Thus, in the case of the common stock of the Wabash Railroad, the present value or cost, aside from temporary speculative manipulation, is measured almost entirely by the voting-power, as there is no immediate prospect of dividend payments of any kind, and the equity back of it is so nebulous and uncertain that it cannot be sanely measured at all. This is also somewhat true of stocks like United States Steel common and Republic Iron; Steel common. While these stocks may temporarily, in an income account, show an apparent earning power, yet when we

The Art of Wall Street Investing
By
John Moody

examine their incomes over a reasonable
period of time, it is usually found that the
value is almost purely speculative, and
that while in prosperous times they may
earn a large surplus, yet in periods of
depression even the dividends on their
preferred stocks are placed in jeopardy.

While common stocks are usually
entitled to all divisible earnings after
payment of interest charges, sinking
funds and preferred dividends, yet there
are exceptions to this rule. In the case of
many railroads, the preferred issues
share certain earnings after the common
has received a given rate. For instance,
the preferred stock of the Chicago,
Milwaukee; St. Paul Railway has a prior
right to 7%; the common then receives
7%, after which each lass shares pro rata
in any further division of profits. There
are other instances of a generally similar
nature, in some cases the common
receiving only one-half of the divisible
surplus over the preferred dividends, the
other half going to the preferred shares
themselves as additional dividends. In
this case a given preferred stock might

The Art of Wall Street Investing
By
John Moody

first receive 6%, then both common and preferred 1% each or more, as the case might be. Consequently, when the common is being paid 6%, the preferred will be receiving 12% per annum.

A preferred stock is a portion of a corporation's capital issue which takes precedence over the remainder, either as to assets or dividends, or both. There are many different characteristics in preferred stock issues ; some have cumulative and some non-cumulative dividend clauses; some have prior security as to assets and some not ; some have exclusive power over the issuing of new mortgages or increases of stock issues and some have not. The Atchison, Topeka; Santa Fe Railway requires that its preferred stock receive 5% non-cumulative dividends; that it have preference over the common shares as to assets (up to its face value), and that no new mortgages or additional preferred stock be issued without the consent of a majority of the holders. By noncumulative is meant that in case the dividend is not paid in a given year, it

The Art of Wall Street Investing
By
John Moody

may be "skipped" entirely, "wiped off the slate," so to speak, and in future only the regular rate need be currently paid before beginning payments on the common stock. It is, therefore, obvious that the non-cumulative clause in a preferred stock is of advantage to the common holder, and may become a decided disadvantage to the preferred holder.

While most railroad preferred stocks are non-cumulative as to dividends, this is not so sweepingly true of industrials. Of eighty-four active industrial preferred stocks described in Moody's Manual for 1905, fifty-eight carry cumulative clauses and twenty-six noncumulative, the proportion of those with cumulative clauses being 66% to the whole. In the case of a cumulative stock all back dividends are regarded as an actual liability, and must be paid before those currently required are satisfied. The result of this is that when the corporation cannot pay the full dividend or any of it, the amount unpaid accumulates as a direct obligation. Many industrial preferred stocks are in arrears on their

The Art of Wall Street Investing
By
John Moody

dividends. Among such at the present time may be mentioned American Can Company preferred (a 7% stock), about 19% in arrears; American Hide and Leather preferred (also 37% stock), 37% in arrears; American Writing Paper Company preferred (7%), 38% in arrears; International Silver preferred, about 20%; United States Cotton Duck Corporation, about 17%. These arrears will all have to be taken care of in some way before the common stocks which follow them can claim any share of the profits. In many cases, arrears of this kind are wiped out by compromise or other capital readjustment. The latter expedient has been adopted in several cases by solvent, money-making corporations, which have found, through an extended experience, that the conditions of their business hardly warrant the heavy dividend charges which the original capitalization proposed. As, under such circumstances it would be practically futile to continue to allow the high dividend charges to accumulate indefinitely, a plan is usually devised to take care of back dividends by

The Art of Wall Street Investing
By
John Moody

a further stock issue or bond issue, and then the cumulative rate is reduced to a figure which the business can reasonably stand. This idea of readjustment is illustrated in a notable manner in the case of the United States Leather Company. This company was actually reorganized and its capitalization entirely transformed for the purpose of financing the accumulations of over 40% of back preferred dividends and to get rid of the high 8% dividend charge for the future.

Stocks are not nearly so heterogeneous as are bond issues. Besides the ordinary stock and the two classes of common and preferred there are comparatively few issues which do not come under these headings. Among these few may be mentioned debenture stock, a special kind of issue popular on some of the Canadian roads, and also on the Chicago Great Western Railway. A debenture stock is generally regarded as being in the same category as a high-grade preferred issue, with usually some kind of special feature to add to its security. As a matter of fact, however, its

The Art of Wall Street Investing
By
John Moody

position and the earnings of the company are the proper measures of its value and not its "debenture" feature. The Chicago Great Western Railway debentures are "guaranteed" to pay 4% interest, the guarantor being the road itself. But this guarantee is not a more binding obligation than would be a cumulative clause in a preferred stock, and if the latter had preference as to its assets, its legal position would be in every way as secure.

In analyzing or judging the value of stocks in general, quite different methods should be employed in the various classes of corporate issues. Stocks of railroads, industrials, tractions, mines, and so forth, while all of the same species, are each of a different genus, and they are all the result of different evolutionary processes. Thus, most of the railroad stocks occupy a much higher plane as investments than do the industrials, and it is generally felt that they are safer and less speculative. This is due to several causes. In the case of

The Art of Wall Street Investing
By
John Moody

the older issues, the railroad properties of
which they are part have greatly
appreciated in value and earning power ;
their territories have grown vastly in
population, and their rights of way,
terminals and other advantages (acquired
many years ago), have all become of
enormous value. While they may have
originally represented little beside
speculation, and their properties may
have been mortgaged "up to the hilt," so
to speak, yet, like the owner of a piece of
land in the heart of a growing city, they
have enjoyed the felicity of seeing an
enormous increment added to the value
of their property over the period which
may have elapsed since the early
speculative days. It was not so many
years since the Delaware. Lackawanna ;
Western Railway was regarded as a
property which, while not very heavily
bonded, would probably never be able to
earn or pay more than a 7% dividend on
its stock issue. It could never become a
fast freight line, nor a through passenger
line like the Pennsylvania or the New
York Central. Indeed, its through

The Art of Wall Street Investing
By
John Moody

connections were not thought to be as good as those of the Erie, and while it was in every way sounder financially than the latter, yet its operating methods were regarded as more or less antiquated and it bore the nickname of "delay, linger and wait." Certainly its future could not equal, it was thought, that of the Central Railroad of New Jersey. And yet, because of the vast growth of population along its line, the great development and concentration of the anthracite coal properties through which it runs, combined with various traffic alliances, the value of the property has appreciated to a point far beyond the wildest visions of those of ten or fifteen years ago. Today the stock of the company is selling at nearly five times its par value, it is paying 10% dividends and earning over 50%, and all this without any material addition of mileage or of acquired properties.

The same tale can be told of nearly all of the older and established lines, though not always to the same degree as in the case of the Delaware, Lackawanna ; Western Railway. There are many newer

The Art of Wall Street Investing
By
John Moody

properties, it is true, where the stocks, and particularly the "common" issues are far more speculative and represent much less tangible property. Thus, there has been a certain amount of modem financing in railroad consolidations, as witness the Rock Island system, the new common stock of which represents practically no tangible property today, and sells at purely speculative prices, even the usual voting power having practically been withheld from it.

Therefore, in judging railroad stocks, these special conditions should be taken into consideration as being the most vital of factors. The railroads all possess special privileges in their rights of way and terminals, which in a country like ours are of constantly growing value because of the swelling population and steady concentration of wealth. It goes without saying that this general tendency will probably be continued for at least several generations' more. Hence, even the least secured railroad stock, unless there are some special disadvantageous features connected with it, will bear

The Art of Wall Street Investing
By
John Moody

examination in this light, for in the course of time, the income will automatically increase with the growth of population and wealth and the stock be benefited thereby.

This principle, however, cannot be so generally applied to industrial stocks. These issues are purely a creation of modern times, as are the great corporations and consolidations which have brought them into being. As is well known, nearly all the newer industrial corporations are greatly over-capitalized, and as a result, the common stocks especially are of a very speculative nature, do not represent anything except voting power and future hopes, and generally sell far below their face values. This condition of things has been brought about by certain apparent necessities in financing, and also because the formation of these great corporations has been of the nature of pure innovation, and the outcome in matters of economy, in methods, in new advantages derived through consolidation and other benefits assumed to be gained by large scale

The Art of Wall Street Investing
By
John Moody

management and production, could not be definitely known or judged until tested over a reasonably long period of time. Therefore the financing of most of these companies has been on a semi-speculative basis, and in order to carry through consolidations and get the necessary financial backing, it has been found necessary to pay very liberal commissions to underwriting syndicates and promoters as well as bankers and others to have the consolidations carried through at all.

The method employed has usually involved the issue of a preferred stock to an amount representing the appraised value of the consolidated plants. As these values have often been actually made higher than the real worth of the properties, there has sometimes resulted a good deal of inflation even in the preferred issue. In addition, a further amount of the preferred stock is then sold for the purpose of raising working capital. When this is not done a bond issue of some kind is usually arranged for this special purpose. A very large issue of

The Art of Wall Street Investing
By
John Moody

common stock is next created and an
.underwriting syndicate undertakes to
pay the face value for all of the preferred
shares not otherwise used in exchange
for plants, property, and so forth,
receiving as its commission for doing this
100% in some cases, and in others as
much as 200%, in common stock. Some
common stock is also issued for the
promoter, perhaps a block is issued to go
to the former owners of the plants and to
other interested parties and for other
special purposes. The syndicate then,
usually through bankers, undertakes to
dispose of the underwritten preferred
stock to investors by giving, as a bonus,
50% to 100% in common stock. The effect
of all this "watering" of the properties is
that the preferred stock is immediately
quoted far below its face value and the
common sells at a very low price; the fact
being that the true value of the properties
may be fairly represented by 80% of the
face value of the preferred and 20% of the
face value of the common. Even if the
preferred stock pays the full dividend
promised (usually 6% or 7%) it will not

The Art of Wall Street Investing
By
John Moody

for a long time appreciate to its par value, and the common of course remains at a very low figure until the earnings actually begin to accumulate to an amount where some kind of definite steady dividend is assured on the common.

In the matter of appreciation through unearned increment, the industrial corporations as a class are not in nearly so fortunate a position as the railroads. In exceptional cases, they have advantages of a high order, which may or may not appreciate; in very few cases have they the certain and fundamental privilege in such large percentage as the railroads. Special legislation may benefit an industrial or it may injure it; tariffs, patents, trade-marks, and so on, will frequently benefit an industrial property, but these are in a sense fixed or stationary advantages, and do not necessarily appreciate in value as do the railroads. The latter have the fundamental advantage of at all times having their feet directly upon the ground. It is true, of course, that the trusts or industrials do finally rest on

The Art of Wall Street Investing
By
John Moody

benefits similar to those of the railroads, which tend to appreciate in the course of time in standing and stability. Thus, coal mining properties, particularly in the limited anthracite field, are in this category ; so are the great realty and construction companies; also the steel and iron manufacturing corporations who own valuable ore and coal deposits, and the oil refineries who also own the original sources of supply. But even these advantages are in a sense uniform and certainly their tendencies to appreciate in value are not to be classed with the more direct tendency shown in the steam railroad properties. Of course in the final analysis, the benefits accruing to transportation companies, also accrue to the benefits of the general class of industrials and will continue so to a greater degree as time goes on, but not for many generations to the point sometimes demanded by the largely inflated issue of common and preferred industrial stocks.

Industrial stocks are either cumulative or non-cumulative and

The Art of Wall Street Investing
By
John Moody

usually carry dividends of either 6% or 7%. The cumulative clauses usually work on the principle already described a few pages back. The dividends are paid quarterly in most cases, but sometimes semiannually. In no cases are dividends supposed to be paid unless actually earned, although there are many instances where a corporation pays a dividend out of accumulated surplus even if not currently earned. It will be readily realized, however, that this kind of policy, if followed to any material extent, cannot be regarded as conservative. No matter how large an accumulated surplus may be, if a growing corporation is currently earning for any length of time only 4% on its capital, it is not sound management to pay out 5%. Where a company begins to do this it should be closely watched.

The Art of Wall Street Investing
By
John Moody

IV

Analyzing Railroad Securities

PROPER judging of the values of railroad securities involves, first of all, the ability to analyze railroad reports. The report of a railroad need not and should not necessarily be left to the study of the expert for analysis, as each investor may, with a reasonable amount of careful training, learn to decipher the statements of the report for himself. While reports are, to the uninitiated, dry and complex affairs, being made up of a number of statistical statements and other groups of figures which seem largely meaningless, yet, as a matter of fact, the salient points in even the most complex and voluminous reports can usually be deciphered at short notice, if one is but familiar with the few fundamental rules

The Art of Wall Street Investing
By
John Moody

which will be explained in the following pages.

As Mr. Thomas F. Woodlock pointed out in his little book, "The Anatomy of a Railroad Report," written over ten years ago, "the object of a railroad report should be to convey an accurate idea of the position of the property, both physical and financial, so that one may know pretty well all the principal circumstances affecting its welfare."

In examining the railroad properties generally, before we consider the securities specifically, we have three distinct divisions of the properties to analyze: first, the physical characteristics; second, the earning power; and third, the financial characteristics. The first and fundamental feature of a railroad property is, of course, the physical. This includes location and length of road; character of territory covered and contiguous to the same; terminal facilities and connections; volume and character of business carried on; volume and description of equipment employed.

The Art of Wall Street Investing
By
John Moody

The second feature to be examined is the income or earning power of the property, and this involves an examination of the company's revenue account, which should cover the following points: Gross earnings, operating expenses, net earnings, income from other sources, fixed charges, dividends and surplus.

The financial characteristics should then be examined. This involves an analysis of the balance sheet, so called, which is always made up of the following four divisions : Capital assets ; current assets ; capital liabilities ; current liabilities.

With the true and proper facts at hand covering the above features, a railroad report can be, after a little experience, analyzed quite simply, and the value of a given security then judged very accurately in connection with it. Nowadays nearly all the railroads of any standing or importance whatever, give practically all of the foregoing facts in their reports in one way or another, and some of them give a great deal more.

The Art of Wall Street Investing
By
John Moody

Where the facts are not given, however, it will usually be found that they can be obtained in the reports of the Interstate Commerce Commission, although the statements of the latter are not given to the public as promptly as one might wish.

I. Physical Characteristics. An examination of this branch of the subject must begin with an examination of the location and length of the road. Every railroad report contains a statement of miles of road, first, second, third and fourth tracks and sidings, and also the mileage operated, controlled and leased or in any other way connected with the company. A complete report should also show in detail, or at least by the aid of a map, the exact location of each division. In the case of the Norfolk ; Western Railway this is done very satisfactorily, thus showing the character of territory through which the road runs. A satisfactory map will also show the connections with other lines, in most cases an item of very great value and importance. These facts, considered in

The Art of Wall Street Investing
By
John Moody

connection with the character of the contiguous and covered territory, are of the first importance. It is a factor of great value to know whether the territory and terminal surroundings are such as to be likely to appreciate in value through general influx of population, development of manufacturing and of agriculture, or the reverse. Valuable characteristics of the Norfolk; Western system are its terminals and connections both east and west. It runs partially through a sparse territory but is one of the soft coal carrying roads, and its branches into the soft coal fields of Virginia and West Virginia are of the first importance, and are likely to grow in value as the years go by, largely because of the characteristic of exclusiveness. The Reading Company's system also enjoys similar characteristics. Its many lines, while enjoying important connection and terminal advantages, would not be in any sense so valuable were it not for its dominating influence in the hard coal fields of Pennsylvania. In controlling the coal output it has a practically exclusive

The Art of Wall Street Investing
By
John Moody

advantage which goes a long way in adding value to its securities. Without this special characteristic it is not at all likely that the Reading Railroad lines would be on anything like the same secure basis that they are today. If the coal fields were accessible to actually competing lines, it is very clear that the Reading Railway earnings would be seriously and permanently affected.

In the matter of terminals and connections, the Reading Company is on a somewhat different basis than the Norfolk; Western. The latter extends from Columbus, Ohio, to Norfolk, Virginia, and the terminals are actually owned by the company. Up to recent years the Reading system had no entrance of its own into New York City, but since 1899 it has controlled the New Jersey Central lines with the latter's important and rapidly appreciating New York terminals. Because of the latter, joined with its Philadelphia terminals and its various alliances with other lines, the Reading properties have shown enormous appreciation in value and earning power

The Art of Wall Street Investing
By
John Moody

during the past few years; and it is clearly evident that the tendency will continue as long as the conditions of control of territory and terminals remain the same. There is practically no factor so important in a railroad property as exclusive rights of way or terminal facilities, or the exclusive control through location, and so forth, of a necessary commodity, such as is anthracite coal in the Eastern states of our country.

It will thus be seen that the location and character of territory of the Norfolk; Western and Reading systems is a factor of great importance, and should be analyzed before anything else. The length of line and character of construction should then be examined, as may very easily be done with the aid of the company reports.

The volume and character of business of course comes under the head of physical characteristics, and should be jointly considered in the examination of the location of the roads. As is well known, the carriage of freight is the important item on every railroad, and the

The Art of Wall Street Investing
By
John Moody

best railroads state in detail the character of tonnage, with the total amount and percentage of each class of freight. The importance of these facts is most obvious.

Where a railroad is dependent for its income largely on some special productive manufacture, such as grain. coal, iron or other special commodities, it is naturally subject to any special condition which may from time to time affect that class of tonnage. Thus, in the case of the coal strike the Reading Company's earnings were very seriously affected ; in the case of a crop failure, such roads as the Northern Pacific, Chicago, Burlington; Quincy or Rock Island would feel the effect to a marked degree. The character of the tonnage, therefore, should be analyzed in connection with its stability, durability and possible fluctuation.

In examining the volume of tonnage, the mere gross amounts of freight carried may mean very little. Traffic density should be ascertained, for both freight and passengers. Most railroad reports

The Art of Wall Street Investing
By
John Moody

give the number of tons carried one mile
and the number of passengers carried
one mile, with the average rate received
per ton and per passenger. By dividing
this ton mileage by the whole number of
miles operated, we get the freight density,
which is the number of tons carried one
mile per mile of road. By the same
method we ascertain the number "'of
passengers carried one mile per mile of
road, this being the passenger density.
Considered together, these two items
make what is known as the traffic
density, and their chief importance lies in
the fact that they show the volume of
business done by the road very closely,
and also enable one to make accurate
comparison with the volume and
character of business done by other
roads. If the proper figures are furnished
it is a comparatively simple matter to
sub-divide the freight density of the
various important classes of traffic.

Train mileage figures are also
important to know. By them is shown the
volume of freight and number of
passengers carried on an average in each

train. Some reports show the average tons and passengers per ton mile, but where they do not they can be ascertained by dividing the tons and passengers carried one mile by the freight and passenger train mileage respectively. A good report should also show the average number of cars empty and loaded in each freight train as well as passengers in each passenger train, and the average amount of freight and number of passengers in each car. These figures are important, especially when examined in comparison with the same figures of previous years, and also with current figures of other roads. If there is a large haulage of empty cars it indicates insufficient equipment or poor management. If the tonnage per train is small, it indicates poor locomotives, bad roadway, weak equipment or short sighted or neglectful management.

By examination in a comparative way of all such figures as these, together with weight of rails, character of road bed, etc., we get at the real physical condition of the road, which is, as

The Art of Wall Street Investing
By
John Moody

pointed out above, a matter of very great moment in an analysis of the property and its securities.

The volume and description of equipment comes under the head of "physical characteristics" also. A good railroad report will show the number of locomotives, their average weight and age, and also the quantity and character of each kind of car owned by the company. These figures are particularly important nowadays and should be given in a clear and exhaustive manner, for the reason that such vast development has taken place in the capacity of locomotives and freight cars during the past few years, that mere numbers may be very misleading. In the matter of coal cars, for instance, great strides have been made in the size and capacity per car, so that a road might today own but 1,000 coal cars, the capacity of which might exceed that of 3,000 cars of twenty years ago. Hence, clear and detailed descriptions of equipment should always be given.

The equipment figures should be studied in comparison with those of

The Art of Wall Street Investing
By
John Moody

previous years in order to be read aright. This is easily done in the cases of the Norfolk; Western and Reading Company reports.

2. Earning Power. Having familiarized oneself with the physical characteristics of a road as outlined in the foregoing pages, the next step for the investor or student to take is to ascertain and then analyze the earning power of the property. This is done through an examination and analysis of the income or revenue account. Every report of course contains such an account, and it is often the most conspicuous statement published in the report. Usually it is too much condensed, but sometimes is presented with satisfactory detail. For the sake of simplicity there is presented below a sample of the usual form, omitting all detail, as applied to a railroad system of 600 miles in length.

The Art of Wall Street Investing
By
John Moody

		Per mile
Gross earnings from operation	$12,000,000	$20,000
Operating expenses	8,000,000	13,333
Net earnings	4,000,000	6,667
Other income	25,0000	417
Total income	4,250,000	7,084
Fixed charges	3,250,000	5,418
Balance	1,000,000	1,666
Dividends	600,000	1,000
Surplus	400,000	666

The income from a railroad is chiefly from operation, but a portion may also arise from interest on investments or loans or income from rentals. The gross income from operation embraces: (a) revenue from passenger transportation ; (b) revenue from freight transportation; (c) revenue from mail, expressage, storage, etc.; (d) revenue from car

The Art of Wall Street Investing
By
John Moody

mileage, switching, etc.; (e) revenue from telegraph companies.

The income from all these items should, of course, be shown in gross, and the laws of the states usually so require it. Rebates, being illegal, should not be included in operating expenses, but should in all cases where they exist be deducted from gross earnings. Such charges as commissions should naturally go into operating expenses. In nearly all reports the revenue from these several different sources is given separately, and the figures are easily understood and compared. There is little room here for mistakes or inaccuracies.

Separate statements of incomes of leased properties should be given in railroad reports having such sources of income, while that of all proprietary branches or lines should naturally be included in the general income account.

Operating expenses is the one item in a railroad report which should always be examined with the greatest care. It is the account most readily manipulated, and through its dissection one can most

The Art of Wall Street Investing
By
John Moody

clearly judge the character and management of the property. To this account the company should charge all expenditures necessary to carry on the business of the road and leave the property at the end of the year in fully as good condition as it was at the beginning of the year. Actual improvements to the property may be charged to the capital or construction account.

Operating expenses are divided into four classes: (a) maintenance of way and structures ; (b) maintenance of equipment ; (c) conducting transportation; (d) general expenses. The Interstate Commerce Commission long ago officially classified operating expenses in this way, and also sub-divided each of these classes into more than fifty sub-divisions.

Maintenance of way and structures, as its title indicates, embraces all charges made in connection with keeping up to the proper standard the roadway, buildings, etc. It is properly divided as follows: (1) repairs of roadway; (2) renewals and repairs of rails and ties; (3)

The Art of Wall Street Investing
By
John Moody

renewals and repairs of stations, crossings, culverts, buildings, bridges, docks, wharves, fences, etc.

Repairs of roadway embraces cost of ballast, clearing of tracks from snow and ice, re-ballasting of tracks and wages and supplies pertaining to this department. Renewals and repairs of rails and ties cover all cost of new rails and ties and the laying of same. Some companies charge to construction account the entire cost of new rails, less the amount for which the old rails may be sold. But this method is not correct. Properly the company should charge to construction account only the amount received for the old rails, the difference being charged to the maintenance account. All railroads find it necessary to replace a certain proportion of rails each year, and this practice should not be neglected. The other items in the maintenance account are largely self-explanatory.

Maintenance of equipment refers entirely to engines and cars. This account should be charged with all money spent to keep the company's rolling stock in

The Art of Wall Street Investing
By
John Moody

fully as good and effective condition as it was at the beginning of the year. Some companies, instead of making proper replacement out of earnings, will allow equipment to depreciate and in time be destroyed and then replace it out of capital account. Companies also sometimes postpone these renewals or repairs. Such customs are to be condemned and careful comparative examinations should be made.

Conducting transportation embraces all expenses incident to hauling or transporting freight or passengers. It includes many items such as salaries and wages of all employees who are engaged in the actual operation of the road, and all supplies used for this particular purpose.

General expenses include salaries of officers, legal expenses, insurance, etc., and, of course, are usually much smaller in amount than the figures in the other divisions mentioned above.

Fixed charges usually include taxes, interest on funded and floating debt, rentals and sinking funds. Taxes should

The Art of Wall Street Investing
By
John Moody

properly be included in operating expenses, but in the majority of cases they are placed in fixed charges. It makes little difference, provided they are clearly and separately stated, but it often misleads the superficial investor if they are not deducted before "net earnings" are announced, as he is prone to forget that the frequently large item of "taxes" must be taken out before interest and dividends. This often happens in examining the monthly and quarterly earnings statements given out to the news agencies and papers by the companies. Interest on funded and floating debt should be stated clearly and in detail, and in connection with it should be given a list of the kinds and amounts of bonds outstanding, with the interest charge thereon, and also, if possible, the character of their particular lien, showing which are prior in security to the others, etc. Rentals should, of course, be stated in detail and so should sinking funds. After all these items are deducted, including special charges, if there are any, the balance is "surplus," the division

The Art of Wall Street Investing
By
John Moody

of which is in the province of the stockholders. It is the net profit of the concern, and out of it are paid the dividends on the stocks of the company. What remains after dividends are deducted is net surplus and is usually added to a "profit and loss" or "surplus income account."

Examination of this "income statement" furnishes the information necessary to know the "earning power" of the railroad. By the reduction to a "per mile basis" comparisons with other roads doing the same class and character of business is readily made.

3. Financial Characteristics. Having familiarized oneself with the physical and earning power of a railroad property, the next step is to examine its financial side. This is taken up through the analysis of the company's balance sheet. Practically nothing can be known of a railroad's financial condition unless the financial statement or balance sheet is carefully examined and dissected.

The balance sheet consists of a statement of the company's assets and liabilities in condensed form. It embraces the following subjects: Capital assets; current assets; capital liabilities; current liabilities; profit and loss, the latter being either a deficit or surplus, as the case may be. Some roads condense their balance sheet entirely too much when inserting it in the annual report while others do not condense enough. In many cases also the mistake is made of not being explicit and clear enough in the insertion of items.

Capital assets consists of: (a) property and franchises, equipment and plant, usually carried under the title of "Cost of road and equipment"; this is commonly known as the construction account ; (b) investments in securities and real estate ; (c) sinking fund accounts.

The construction account is supposed to represent the total amount of capital invested in the road and its equipment. It is frequently the case, however, that certain other items, such as discounts on securities sold, are charged to this account. This account

The Art of Wall Street Investing
By
John Moody

also usually takes care of special charges and expenses made in the financing of capital issues, reorganizations of the property, and so forth. The account is in a sense rather an elastic one and the charges in it are capable of great misuse. Properly the railroad should itemize the charges which are made to this account during the year, in order that the stockholders may know exactly how to account for the increases which may appear. If this v/ere always done it would not be possible for any railroad management to juggle with this account as is sometimes done. There have been instances in the past where the construction account has been made the receptacle for all sorts of items representing little or no value. For instance, in the case of the old Atchison Railroad, reorganized in 1895, it was found that out of a construction account carried in the balance sheet at over $95,000,000, more than $40,000,000 represented nominal entries such as discounts on bonds, reorganization expenses, etc.

The Art of Wall Street Investing
By
John Moody

"Investments in securities or real estate" is not as clearly shown in most railroad reports as it should be. All the large roads own various stocks and bonds of other roads, which have been acquired in many ways; sometimes by direct purchase or control, by original subscription, by exchange of securities, or in payment of advances made or construction work done. If these items were made explicit enough it would be a comparatively easy matter to ascertain whether they were being carried at too high a valuation in the balance sheet. In addition to this, it is necessary to compare these items in connection with the item on income from investments in the income account. It can be fairly well ascertained by such a comparison what the real value of the investments are and whether they are overvalued in the balance sheet. There are cases, of course, where one railroad property will acquire, for control in a strategic sense, the securities of another property and not merely for the income to be derived directly therefrom.

The Art of Wall Street Investing
By
John Moody

But when this is the case, it is usually so evident that it is not necessary to have it stated explicitly.

Sinking funds should be shown in the balance sheet in detail; showing each kind of sinking fund and bond separately. Car trust payments, where there are any, should be treated in the same general manner.

The current assets of a company include all movable and changeable assets excepting material supplies, which may be in use for the purpose of liquidating the general business debts of the company, independent of the capital assets. The main headings under current assets are : (a) cash on hand and on deposit ; (b) loans and bills receivable ; (c) accounts receivable; (d) due from other companies and individuals; (e) due from companies, agents and officers; (f) advances to other companies; (g) sundry assets.

The item "cash," of course explains itself. Loans and bills receivable is not ordinarily a large account. It represents money owed by shippers for freight

The Art of Wall Street Investing
By
John Moody

transported, and so forth, and may also represent loans made by the road or notes held by the road. If the item of "loans" increases from year to year it is not a good thing, unless there are special reasons given for it. "Accounts receivable" explain themselves, as does the item due from other companies and individuals. "Advances to other companies," if large, should be carefully examined. It may mean money loaned by the company to some weak, struggling allied company whose bonds may be guaranteed by the main company, or of which control is held in some way. These advances may be small and therefore only nominal, but if they continue to grow it may mean that the parent company is advancing money which may never come back to it at all. The chief importance of the item lies in the change it may produce on the other side of the balance sheet.

The items, "due from agents and officers," and "sundry assets," explain themselves. The smaller they are kept from month to month and year to year, the healthier the condition of the road is apt to be.

"Capital liabilities" consists of stocks and bonds only. There are several kinds of stock and many kinds of bonds which require no description here, as they have been especially considered in Chapters II and III. The balance sheet should show the actual amount of capital stock outstanding, whether owned by the company or not. If the company has any of this stock in its treasury, this latter should be shown as an asset on the other side of the balance sheet. The various kinds of bonds should be separately shown, the actual amount outstanding being given in each case. By comparing these amounts with those of previous years, the changes and increases can be readily ascertained. In most railroad reports, separate detailed statements are furnished describing the funded debt, and in some cases showing the actual property on which the different mortgages are secured.

"Current liabilities" are made up of several important items which usually come under the following heads: (a) loans and bills payable; (b) accounts payable ; (c) pay rolls and vouchers; (d) interest and dividends accrued; (e) due to other companies; (f) sundry liabilities. These items are generally sub-divided into "floating debt" and ^'operating liabilities." The "operating liabilities" are generally purely current, and do not usually represent more than one or two months items. If they extend much beyond this, it is often the case that the road is running behind and its management is in a bad way. The important item to be examined in current liabilities is "loans and bills payable." If this item is small and does not grow from year to year it may mean very little. If it does grow, however, it usually means that the company is borrowing money temporarily for construction or improvements which it intends to take care of with some permanent security, such as stock or bonds; later on. If this is not the case and no new work is being undertaken, then it surely means that there will be trouble ahead. It is better if a railroad has no

The Art of Wall Street Investing
By
John Moody

loans or bills payable, and in normal times a well-managed property will not allow this item to expand, even if it is doing a good deal of building. It will generally be found more economical to finance its capital requirements as it goes along.

The item "accounts payable" is not significant unless it shows rapid increase in amount. This is also true of other items, such as payrolls and vouchers, traffic balances, etc. The item "interest or dividends accrued" is generally off-set by "current assets" on the other side of the balance sheet.

In addition to the items in the balance sheet mentioned above there is always the one item of "profit and loss," or "surplus," which is always found on the liability side, when the company is in sound condition. Theoretically, it represents an actual surplus, but as a matter of fact, it does not always represent this, as the money supposed to be contained in the account is usually absorbed somewhere else in the accounts of the company.

The Art of Wall Street Investing
By
John Moody

In the foregoing chapter the chief points in a railroad report have been referred to. Very few railroads give all the essential facts as clearly as they should; this being particularly true of the physical characteristics. There are, however, various ways by which the investor can ascertain many facts regarding the physical status of a railroad outside of an annual report. As for the financial statistics, it is nowadays a comparatively simple matter for anyone to secure the necessary facts regarding any railroad in the country, large or small, through the Interstate Commerce Commission of Washington. The only drawback of this method is that the reports of the Department are not made up promptly enough for the use of many prospective investors.

V

Tractions and Industrials

THE investment market for industrial
and, traction securities has undergone a
vast development in Wall Street during
the past half dozen years. Previous to
that time a thorough discussion of Wall
Street could be made without any
particular reference to this subject, but
nowadays a large proportion of the
transactions there are in either industrial
securities or those of the various public
service corporations. There are certain
features underlying traction or other
franchise corporation securities which do
not affect railroad securities to any
extent. It is true that steam railroads are
in a broad sense "franchise" corporations,
but the franchise is not the important
feature as it is in the case of a street

The Art of Wall Street Investing
By
John Moody

railway, gas, electric light or water company. In the promoting or developing of any of these the franchise is regarded as the fundamental thing and without it no company can operate at all.

In the case of the street railway the franchise does not usually merely authorize the company to construct a railroad through a piece of property after it has bought that property, as does the steam railroad franchise, but it conveys to the corporation the exclusive right to operate over public property for a certain term of years ; perhaps for an unlimited period of time. A franchise of this kind does not merely give a company a legal right to construct and operate, but it gives it a more or less exclusive right; and on the value of this privilege, whatever it may be, depends entirely the value of the securities which are built upon it. In examining, from the investor's standpoint, the bonds or stock of a franchise or public utility corporation, we should before all else examine the franchise. To do this we must ascertain its length, its scope, the terms or

The Art of Wall Street Investing
By
John Moody

conditions of its renewal, and its limitations, if it has any. We must also bear in mind and carefully weigh the character of the community which grants the franchise, and not overlook the possible effect of change in public sentiment. While a city or other municipality cannot as a rule cancel a franchise which has been legally granted, and with the terms of which the company has complied, yet there are methods whereby the community can, if it so elect, take to itself, through taxation, what is generally termed the "unearned increment" in the franchise. For instance, a city may by legislation limit the rate of fare which the company may be allowed to charge; it may insist upon a transfer system which will tend to reduce the income of the railroad; it may adopt a franchise tax law requiring the company to pay into the city's treasury a certain proportion of its earnings in addition to the amount paid for ordinary taxes. This feature of the franchise question is coming to the front very rapidly nowadays and it is quite necessary for the

The Art of Wall Street Investing
By
John Moody

intelligent investor to be thoroughly informed along this line.. ,The franchise corporations are purely modern institutions, and, like the industrials, have nearly all been organized on a more or less inflated basis. For instance, the various properties owned and controlled by the New Jersey Public Service Corporation are capitalized for over $210,000,000, and yet they could probably be replaced, aside from the franchise values, for less than $80,000,000. The difference, of course, is supposed to represent the actual value of the franchises, and as these values are in most cases very tangible and growing rapidly, it is claimed that they should be represented by a reasonable amount of securities. The danger in this argument, however, from the investor's standpoint, lies in the fact that the communities themselves all retain the taxing power and have a perfect right, if public opinion so elects, to tax into the public treasury the entire value of these franchises. Should this program be generally pursued throughout the

The Art of Wall Street Investing
By
John Moody

country it will readily be seen that both bonds and stocks of traction and other public service companies which merely represent this current franchise value, will largely evaporate into nebulous ether.

Industrial securities are similar to tractions in many ways. They also depend more or less on a franchise right or on some special legislation, which gives them a benefit which they have capitalized. In the case of the United States Steel Corporation, for instance, not only has the actual cost of the manufacturing properties been fully capitalized, but the company has issued large amounts of securities to represent the estimated values of its ore and coal lands ten or twenty years in the future and has also capitalized in a very liberal manner the special benefits which it enjoys because of protective tariff legislation, patent rights, shipping facilities, contracts, etc. These things, while apparently permanent enough at the present time, are still not fundamental values and can easily be removed through the force of public

The Art of Wall Street Investing
By
John Moody

sentiment. Not only may these special advantages be removed, but the people may someday decide to clap heavy taxes on ore, coal and other lands now taxed but lightly.

This is not true, however, of the steam railroad advantages, which are chiefly made up of rights of way and terminals which originally were of not much importance, but which have shown enormous appreciation in value because of the great influx of population and general development of the country during recent decades. While the steam railroads are to a degree subject to legislative regulation and taxation, yet the special advantages which they enjoy are so much more firmly secured than those of the traction and industrial companies, that danger of any real and serious disturbance of these advantages is comparatively remote. It is true that sentiment is growing more or less rapidly nowadays in favor of government control or ownership of steam railroads, but it is not likely that the latter will be brought about in a way which will be particularly detrimental to the interest of the holders of anything but the most inferior classes of railroad securities. Masses of traction and industrial securities are vulnerable because of the fact that such a large proportion of them are based on purely speculative foundations, while the majority of railroad securities represent much more real value, which has been created in one way or another over a longer period of time, and is much more certain of permanency.

In judging industrial and traction securities, therefore, the methods which have been outlined in other chapters for the analysis of steam railroad securities should be applied only in a very qualified sense. The features pointed out above should be constantly borne in mind as the most important factors which are likely to affect the present or future values of the securities.

The Art of Wall Street Investing
By
John Moody

VI
Investment versus Speculation

THERE are two classes of people in Wall Street who invest money in securities. One class consists of actual investors. The actual investor is the man who invests for him-self and buys securities to keep. He either does this directly or does it through a bond dealer or other broker in securities. When the dealer buys securities he has certain motives which the investor himself has not, and in making his purchases takes certain other factors into consideration. The individual investor does not give much thought to the temporary condition of the market, and it does not matter much to him what the temporary course of prices may be. But the broker or bond dealer must not only take into consideration the intrinsic value of the investment itself, but he must also consider the condition of the money market, and of various other factors of a more or less temporary

The Art of Wall Street Investing
By
John Moody

nature which may affect the price of the security. In other words, he must buy as cheaply as he can, for the simple reason that he is not an investor and buys simply for the purpose of turning over the security at a profit to someone else.

The distinction between these two men indicates the cardinal distinction between the investor and the speculator. While the bond dealer is not a speculator in the commonly accepted sense, yet his motive is, in a more limited and conservative way, of the same nature as that of the speculator. The latter buys to make a profit on the principal. The investor buys to secure an income; that is to say, he places his money in what he thinks or is led to believe is an absolutely secure piece of property, and he has no other purpose in view than that of receiving a current return upon it in the shape of interest or dividends. Such is the pure investor, while the pure speculator is one who pays no attention to dividends and interest as an income, but is actuated entirely with the idea of profit on principal. Of course, there are

The Art of Wall Street Investing
By
John Moody

many men who are both investors and
speculators, and a large number follow
the practice of putting money in what are
known as semi-speculative investments.
A semi-speculative investment is one
which furnishes an income in the shape
of dividends or interest, and at the same
time is supposed to promise a reasonable
appreciation in principal over a certain
period of time. For instance, the man who
puts money into a stock like the United
States Steel preferred, might reasonably
be called a semi-speculative investor. He
invests not merely to get a liberal
dividend, but has a theory that as the
stock is not selling very high there may
be a fair chance for appreciation in the
principal, in the event of which he will
sell out and re-invest his money with the
profit made in some other security. While
this method has proven successful in
many cases, yet there is necessarily a
large element of speculation in it when
carried to an extreme, for if a serious
mistake is made by the investor, a large
proportion of his principal may be wiped
out, and in this case he will quickly find

The Art of Wall Street Investing
By
John Moody

that it would have been much wiser for him to have confined himself entirely to securities which have no speculative value, but are bought and sold entirely on an investment basis.

In addition to pointing out the distinction between investing and speculating in Wall Street, it is worthwhile to also show the line between speculating and what is commonly known as gambling in stocks. The man who speculates in stocks acts on information which he has ascertained and analyzed in one way or another. To be sure, his judgment may be entirely at fault, but he generally has a plausible business reason for buying or selling such and such a security. For instance, he may have made up his mind that a certain railroad stock is selling too low in view of current earnings and immediate prospects, such, for instance as the crop outlook, and based on this he may decide to buy for a rise. This is generally known as a "speculation." A "gamble," on the other hand, is where a man buys and sells on a blind chance, without any

The Art of Wall Street Investing
By
John Moody

particularly sane reason, except that he thinks that a turn in the market up or down is due, or that the pools and "big fellows" mean to give a twist to the stock. A large portion of the gambling is done in bucket shops, but a respectable amount of it also finds its way into the offices of the larger brokers and commission dealers. There are a limited number of men who gamble in stocks on a very large scale and sometimes make as well as lose very large amounts of money. This is also true of the speculative market, and nowadays actual speculation in stocks is carried on at an enormous scale, the speculative leaders in many cases being some of the most prominent men in the Street. The great aggregate of speculation is made up of these men with their many thousands of smaller followers in all parts of the country.

The Art of Wall Street Investing
By
John Moody

VII

" Get-Rich-Quick "
Schemes

THERE are many methods in vogue for inducing people to part with their money, but the most effective way to interest a certain very considerable portion of the American public in propositions the ultimate purpose of which is the separation of the individual from his property, is through what is known in Wall Street as the "get-rich-quick" scheme. It is an old saying that the American public likes to be fooled, and judging from the way these many fraudulent schemes keep bobbing into sight with never ending regularity, it would seem that the saying has lost none of its truthfulness.

There are get-rich-quick schemes of many kinds, and they are exploited in many ways; sometimes through the columns of newspapers, sometimes in

The Art of Wall Street Investing
By
John Moody

financial or mining journals, but more often through circulars or other advertising matter. The most successful are usually mining propositions, although many other kinds have flourished equally as well. One of the most notorious promotion frauds of this kind was a "guaranteed egg company," the stock of which was offered for sale in New York City a few years ago. The promoters of this company sent broadcast a roseate prospectus, offering the sale of 7% guaranteed preferred stock at par, with a large bonus in common stock. Careful inspection of the prospectus revealed the fact that the prospective earnings, which were to amount to a fabulous sum, were to result from the sale of eggs at high prices, the said eggs to be laid without fail at a certain unceasing rate by several thousand hens, which were the entire stock in trade of the company. These hens were supposed to do the double work of hatching new broods of chickens and at the same time laying their regular guaranteed proportion of eggs. It was also assumed that only hens and not roosters

The Art of Wall Street Investing
By
John Moody

would be hatched and that every egg would be good. The essence of the "guarantee" on the preferred stock appeared to be wholly based on the theory that the hens had somehow been forced into a promise to lay eggs night and day, if need be, in order not to allow the preferred stock dividends to lapse in any possible way. The company was capitalized in the neighborhood of a million dollars and its only tangible property, aside from the chickens, was a farm of twenty acres located about thirty miles from New York.

Absurd as this whole proposition was, there were enough investing idiots walking around loose in New York City to "nibble" at this bait to the extent of over $80,000 in cash. And it was stated on good authority that most of these subscriptions came from New York City people who had never seen a chicken farm in their lives, and probably didn't know any more about the chicken and hen laying business than the chickens themselves knew about the preferred stock they were assumed to be

The Art of Wall Street Investing
By
John Moody

guaranteeing the dividends on. Shortly after this exploitation, the promoters quietly folded their tents and stole away, as certain kinds of promoters have a way of doing, with the result that the innocent but superficial investors are still waiting for their dividends, and are holding their stocks as "permanent investments."

Another instance of the get-rich-quick scheme which fooled a large number of supposedly sane investors was the promotion of the "sea water gold" enterprise a few years ago. A certain man named Jergensen, who was more avaricious than honest, happened to discover an article in an encyclopedia which brought to his knowledge the fact that sea water contains a small percentage of gold, but that no method has ever been discovered whereby the separation of the two could be brought about. He then devised a scheme for pretending that he had himself invented a secret process for doing this very thing, and thereby induced investors to pass their ready cash his way. He built a small plant on the water's edge at South Lubec,

The Art of Wall Street Investing
By
John Moody

Maine, a portion of the plant being constructed out of sight, and under water. He then secured a small quantity of gold bullion (a small genuine gold brick) and exhibited it to certain people in the city of Boston, at the same time making the statement that it was the result of a test of his secret process for washing gold from sea water. His incredulous listeners were invited to go to the government assay office with him to test the genuineness of the little brick. This they did and to their surprise found that it was all pure gold. Then, as a further proof of his discovery, Jergensen invited them to go to South Lubec with him and see his plant. They did so and saw the mysterious looking machinery, part of which was under water. They were duly impressed. He then explained that he could not let them see how he did it, as he must naturally guard his secret. But the next morning he appeared with a small can full of new gold dust, which he said he had secretly washed out during the night. After that, for a whole week, while his visitors remained, he appeared

The Art of Wall Street Investing
By
John Moody

every morning with a moderate quantity of gold dust which he exhibited as a result of the previous night's work« As this production steadily continued his audience grew. Others came on from Boston and the wonderful discovery was on the lips of a steadily increasing number of people. When he next went to Boston, taking the gold dust with him, and converted it into cash at the assay office, many apparently shrewd people were thoroughly convinced and regarded his claims as absolutely proven. He then organized a company and began to sell stock, and as the snowball had begun to roll, it very quickly increased to gigantic proportions.

Within a short period, investors in Boston and vicinity were sacrificing good bonds and stocks, withdrawing savings bank deposits, and generally falling over each other in a mad rush to get in on the ground floor in this sea water gold bonanza. It was afterwards estimated that before the fraud was publicly exposed, Jergensen and his accomplices had secured nearly a million dollars. The

The Art of Wall Street Investing
By
John Moody

final outcome was, that Jergensen secretly escaped to Europe with most of the money, and his victims are whistling for their "great profits" to this day.

Many other schemes equally as fraudulent have been worked during recent years in Wall Street and elsewhere, and though constantly exposed in the newspapers, yet new ones crop up nearly every day, and the public continue to bite. The advertising columns of the newspapers and magazines are full to overflowing with roseate propositions for the investment of money; gold and copper mines; industrial undertakings; new railroad projects; traction companies, and various other promotion schemes. Millions of dollars are invested every week by small investors in this country, and a large proportion of it is constantly "steered" into unsafe channels, with a resultant loss to thousands of investors. As an illustration of how persistently and easily unsuspecting people are misled and swindled, instance the following: A very conspicuous concern has been "operating for the past five years or so

The Art of Wall Street Investing
By
John Moody

one of the largest and cleverest mining swindles ever known in the United States. Sumptuous offices are maintained in Broadway, New York, and about forty branch offices have been established in various cities of the United States and Canada. A number of honest men have been drawn into the scheme by baits of alluring commissions, and have peddled the rotten shares of this firm of stock-jobbers among their friends and neighbors, to the loss of their own peace of mind and reputations. The plan of this swindle is neat and comprehensive. The firm announced that it would operate on the law of averages, and by handling many mines the good ones would make up for the failures. Considerable bluffing has been done in the way of crude mining operations, but none of the 'mines' have proven successful, and none are likely ever to be successful.

"This firm of sharpers began paying dividends on shares, when no profits were earned, for which they should be jailed for the common swindlers that they are. Stock in the worthless companies

The Art of Wall Street Investing
By
John Moody

were exchanged for stock in equally worthless companies whenever shareholders grew tired, and the victims of conspiracy were tolled along by the 'dividends' paid out of the money they had themselves furnished. Recently cash dividends have been suspended, and 'scrip' dividends substituted therefore. It is reported that this firm has bilked something like 16,000 small investors, in the United States and Canada, to the tune of several millions of dollars."

The methods for promoting all kinds of swindles have in recent years been refined down to an exact science. Experience has proven that the most vulnerable class of people to be attracted by investing swindles aside from women, are ministers, doctors, teachers and other professional people. There are in New York a number of concerns who make a business of supplying classified lists of possible investors for the use of those who wish to exploit mining swindles and other schemes. These lists are classified into ten dollar investors, twenty-five to one hundred dollar investors, one

The Art of Wall Street Investing
By
John Moody

hundred to five hundred dollar investors; and investors having $10,000 or more available. The "ten dollar investors" are mostly made up of a class of people who are in the habit of taking a small "flyer" occasionally of not over ten dollars, investing this amount on the theory that it may turn out with a big profit, but that in any event the loss cannot exceed ten dollars. This class appeals to the swindler also, in spite of the fact that the amounts invested are so small, for the reason that even if the scheme is exposed as a swindle, the individual amounts are so small that it would not pay any single person to resort to law for the recovery of his money. True it is that a large number of such investors, if acting in concert, would become a menace, but as a rule such investors are too widely scattered, or too unintelligent or indifferent to make any move of this kind. In number, these ten dollar investor lists run into the hundred thousands, and are the main avenue for floating all schemes of the cheaper and more openly fraudulent variety.

The Art of Wall Street Investing
By
John Moody

The "twenty-five to fifty dollar" list is made up of country investors, Methodist and Baptist ministers, country doctors and all classes of teachers ; also barbers, waiters, hospital nurses and the general class of people who are able in one way or other to set aside for a rainy day from $25 to $100 per year. These lists are used in slightly more pretentious schemes, of course, with sometimes a little more merit to them. The $100 to $500 investors consist of doctors of slightly higher grade than those referred to above; also college teachers and professors, small Wall Street lambs, Episcopal and Presbyterian ministers, mercantile clerks, some country merchants and other thrifty people who annually accumulate a few hundred dollars over and above their cost of living. Such lists are used for more pretentious schemes, and, in addition to the promotion of frauds, they are sometimes used in perfectly sound and legitimate enterprises. The higher grade lists, covering $1,000 to $100,000 investors, largely explain themselves, and while they are as often used by schemers

The Art of Wall Street Investing
By
John Moody

for offering their wares, yet as they are largely made up of more sensible and cautious people, they are not so popular in the "get-rich-quick" promoting fraternity of the larger lists of more modest investors.

While swindles are promoted to a gigantic extent through circulars and by mail, yet much business is also done through the medium of newspapers, magazines, and so forth. Many (but not all) of the large metropolitan dailies will sell advertising space in which notorious swindles are promoted ; magazines also of high-grade in other ways, constantly sell space for the exploitation of mining, real estate and other schemes; the columns of country dailies and weeklies are not only open as a rule to such schemes, but for a consideration they will often publish "write-ups" recommending or booming a particular enterprise. The "write-ups" generally consist of editorial or other special articles which are prepared or endorsed by the promoters themselves, and they of course pass in

The Art of Wall Street Investing
By
John Moody

the reader's mind as genuine and truthful.

These are, of course, frauds of the most palpable kind and the publication of such matter is entirely unfair to the readers of the paper. It is a species of cheap and insidious deception which should, wherever found, be condemned in unmeasured terms. Another illegitimate method of the promotion of swindles is through trade journals, particularly in the mining industry. This country is nowadays flooded with mining newspapers and journals, which, while ostensibly independent and legitimate in their character and methods, are, as a matter of fact, actually owned and controlled by the same people who are engaged in the promotion of mining and other swindles on a gigantic scale. These journals are filled with special articles and editorials which recommend and describe in glittering terms, the stocks and possibilities of this and that enterprise in mining, or oil, or real estate, or manufacturing, in which they themselves are interested. This is a more

The Art of Wall Street Investing
By
John Moody

modern method of exploiting swindles than some of the others, and apparently has been most effective.

In considering roseate prospectuses and the various other plans which are constantly found in the public prints offering shares for sale, one of the rules of nearly universal application, which will usually go a long way toward the protection of the investor, is this: Always question any proposition offering stocks or bonds for sale where such offers are made directly by the company itself, and not through a banking house or other reputable concern. If no bankers are handling the sale of securities it is usually the case that there is something "shady" about the scheme. There are exceptions, of course, but not many. If the securities are offered by bankers and brokers, the next step should be to ascertain the standing, reputation and financial strength of the bankers or brokers themselves. Wall Street and the other financial centers of the country have their full share of irresponsible concerns of this class.

The Art of Wall Street Investing
By
John Moody

The apparently plausible statement is frequently made that money is saved to the company and its stockholders by avoiding the employment of a banker or agent to market securties. But this is not so in ninety-nine cases out of a hundred. If a proposition has merit, the promoters always find it much more economical to go to a concern who have specialized and have developed the proper machinery for the floating of securities, rather than undertake to do it themselves. The banker not only has the clientele, but he has the organization for handling the business effectively and economically; and, of course, in many cases his prestige and general reputation have much to do with making the flotation a success. For all this he frequently charges a good round commission; sometimes too much, perhaps, but not so often as is generally supposed. Indeed, it would in most cases upon investigation prove to be a fact that without the banking medium, the flotation would cost far more than the usual amount represented by an apparently heavy discount or

The Art of Wall Street Investing
By
John Moody

commission. It is a part of the business of the banker to float securities, just as it is a part of the business of the trust company to pay coupons. People sometimes think it strange that a large corporation, with an office in New York City, should pay a commission to a trust company to cash the coupons on its own bonds each six months, when it apparently might do this work itself. But the answer to that is that the trust company maintains the machinery and organization for paying the coupons of not merely one but of perhaps one hundred companies, and therefore can afford to do such work at a minimum cost and for far less than the corporation itself could possibly do it.

It will be seen, after reading the foregoing chapter, that the simplest and quickest way of avoiding the "get-rich-quick" scheme, no matter where or how presented or however roseate and plausible its promises and claims may be, is to never entertain any proposition which is not offered through a banker or other agent, and then, having adopted this rule, to go one step further: never have dealings with a banker, broker or financial agent until you have investigated and are satisfied as to his character, standing and general reputation.

VIII

Reorganizations and Syndicates

THE subject of reorganizations is, of course, too wide a one to treat adequately in a book of limited size and scope such as this, and it is only practicable to touch upon it briefly. Reorganizations in both railroad and industrial finance are brought about as a result of various causes; one of the chief being over-capitalization. In the period extending from 1893 to 1897, a large number of the most important railroad systems of the country were reorganized, and their capitalizations scaled down very extensively, — in some cases more than fifty per cent. In the same period many of the larger industrial combinations were also reorganized, the chief among these being the well-known Cordage Trust.

The Art of Wall Street Investing
By
John Moody

It sometimes happens that a concern is reorganized for other reasons than insolvency. Thus, the Standard Oil Trust was reorganized, being changed from a trusteed aggregation of separate companies to one large corporation of $97,500,000 capital. This change was made to conform to newly enacted laws, and as a partial concession to public sentiment. A concrete example of the methods and purpose as well as the anticipated results of reorganization can best be shown in the manner followed below. In this way we will avoid the complexity which always results in analyzing an actual reorganization with its many details, whereas by creating a simple example as is done below, we demonstrate the principle without beclouding the mind of the student with incidental facts and figures.

Let us assume the existence of a railroad system of 1,500 miles, known as the Great Southern Railroad Company. It is capitalized as follows:

The Art of Wall Street Investing
By
John Moody

First Mortgage 6% bonds, due 1920	$3,000,000
Second Mortgage, 5% bonds, due 1935	3,000,000
Consolidated Mortgage 5% bonds, due	
1950	2,000,000
Preferred Stock (6% cumulative)	3,000,000
Common Stock	3,000,000
Total capitalization (par value)	$14,000,000

It will be noted that to pay the interest on the three bond issues requires $430,000 per year, and if 6% is also paid on preferred stock, $180,000 additional will be required, making $610,000 in all. To pay any dividend on the common stock would, of course, require a still further amount.

Now let us assume also that the first mortgage carries a sinking fund of $60,000 per year, which must be covered,

The Art of Wall Street Investing
By
John Moody

of course, out of earnings. This will increase the total charges to $90,000 per annum, excluding the dividend charge.

Over a period of six years the gross and net earnings of this road have resulted as follows :

Gross Earnings		Operating Expenses	Net Earnings	Fixed Charges	Difference
1900.	$2,000,000	$1,300,000 (65%)	$700,000	$490,000	$210,000+
1901.	2,100,000	1,366,000 (65%)	735,000	490,000	245,000+
1902.	1,600,000	1,120,000 (65%)	480,000	490,000	10,000-
1903.	1,800,000	1,080,000 (60%)	720,000	490,000	230,000+
1904.	1,050,000	735,000 (70%)	315,000	490,000	175,000-
1905.	1,400,000	1,050,000 (75%)	350,000	490,000	140,000-

(In the last column the plus (+) sign indicates surplus, and the minus (-) sign deficit.)

In examining the foregoing statement we note that in 1900 and 1901 the road earned a comfortable surplus over charges, and we can assume that a part of this surplus was paid out in preferred stock dividends. The road was pretty heavily bonded but it was operated on the theory that growing business would take care of these heavy

The Art of Wall Street Investing
By
John Moody

requirements. But in the third year, a very serious falling off in earnings occurred, owing to a crop failure, and the net earnings were not quite equal to the charges. In the fourth year, however, a substantial recovery is made and a good surplus again shown. But in the fifth and sixth years further serious reverses occur and vast deficits are shown. In the endeavor to keep down expenses during these latter years, the roadbed has not been properly taken care of, equipment has run down at the heel, and the property has been "skinned" generally in order to show net results. It will be noted that in the earlier years the percentage of expenses to gross, even when the latter totals were larger, was 65%, a normal figure. But later, when the gross began to drop, the expenses were cut down in even greater proportion (except in 1904, when the gross fall was extraordinarily heavy) and practically no money was spent on the property to keep it up to the proper standard for doing business. The net result is that when 1905 arrives, the company is in a disastrous condition ;

The Art of Wall Street Investing
By
John Moody

and has not even available funds to meet its charges, not to mention money needed for absolutely necessary expenditures to maintain the property. Besides, its credit is gone, its securities are selling at great discounts, and it is in no position to raise new capital. Its only course is to apply to the courts for a receiver, which it does. The receiver then takes charge and operates the property, pending its reorganization.

After certain examinations and delays, committees representing bondholders and stock-holders get together, and in time a plan of reorganization is formulated and united upon. In this particular case the plan might reasonably be worked out, along the following lines:

A new company is formed with an authorized capital as follows:

Common stock	$ 5,000,000
Preferred stock (4% non-cumulative)	2,000,000
First Consol. 4% bonds	10,000,000
Total	$17,000,000

The Art of Wall Street Investing
By
John Moody

The old second mortgage bondholders are then offered an equal amount ($3,000,000) of the new consol. 4% bonds in exchange for their holdings; the old consolidated holders are offered 50% ($1,000,000) in new consol. 4% bonds and 50% ($1,000,000) in new 4% preferred stock; the old preferred stockholders are offered 20% ($600,000) in new 4% preferred stock and 80% ($2,400,000) in new common stock; the old common stockholders are required to pay an assessment of 10% ($300,000) after which they receive $10 per share in new preferred stock and $30 per share ($1,800,000) in new common stock. If this plan is carried through to a success the net results after completion will be as follows:

There will be outstanding —

Old First Mortgage 6% bonds (undisturbed)	$3,000,000
New Consol. Mortgage 4% bonds	4,000,000
New Preferred stock	1,900,000
New Common stock	4,200,000
Total	$13,100,000

The Art of Wall Street Investing
By
John Moody

There will be left unissued $6,000,000 of the new 4% consols, of which $3,000,000 will be reserved to retire the old first mortgage 6s when the latter mature, and the balance will be reserved for capital requirements. With the preferred and common stock not disposed of in the above statement ($100,000 in preferred and $800,000 in common), the reorganization committee and underwriting syndicates will be compensated for their work and reimbursed for their expenses. The total capitalization outstanding therefore, when the reorganization is completed, will be $14,000,000, exactly the same as was the case with the old company.

Note, however, the changes that have been brought about; The reorganized company has received $300,000 in new cash and also has $3,000,000 of available 4% bonds in its treasury (a portion of which may be underwritten in the plan and sold immediately for use in improving the property) , and its fixed charges, including the old sinking fund, will have

The Art of Wall Street Investing
By
John Moody

been reduced from $490,000 to $400,000 per annum. As the average annual net earnings of the property for the six year period were $550,000, the road is now in a financial position where it can immediately show a substantial surplus above its charges. Under the new regime, with gross earnings at $1,700,000 (the average for six years) and assuming average operating expenses of 66 2-3%, we would have a surplus above charges of $166,666, which would equal, besides the 4% dividends on the preferred stock, nearly 2% on the common stock. In the event of some of the treasury bonds being issued for improvements or acquisitions it would, of course, probably result that an equivalent increase in income would be shown.

It is in the carrying through of a plan just as the foregoing, that the work of the underwriting syndicate comes in. The syndicate consists of a group of financiers bankers or others of financial standing and resourcefulness, who band together and formally agree to guarantee the success of the plan. Usually a

The Art of Wall Street Investing
By
John Moody

banking house or trust company of prominence becomes the syndicate manager. An agreement is then entered into by the syndicate to take all the bonds and stocks at a given price which are not taken by the original holders themselves on the terms of the plan. In this way the success of the plan is insured, and the old holders who refuse to join in the reorganization are either given their money or bought out on a mutually satisfactory basis.

The underwriting syndicate seeks its profit in two ways. First, through a commission from the new company, which usually comes in the shape of securities. In the foregoing case the syndicate would get $100,000 in preferred stock and $800,000 in common stock. Second, the syndicate expects, as an additional source of income, to sell at a profit through its syndicate managers, whatever securities it is obliged to take up in the underwriting. If these securities are not marketable, they are then either "tied up" and carried for a certain specified period, with a view of ultimate

The Art of Wall Street Investing
By
John Moody

sale, or else they are delivered directly to the members of the syndicate, who do what they see fit with them.

Within the past ten years, and particularly since the great expansion of corporate enterprise in both the railroad and industrial fields, the so-called syndicate underwriting business has grown to a position of great importance in Wall Street. There are certain concerns of large capital and resources who do practically nothing else. It goes without saying therefore, that the underwriting syndicate is a necessary part of the Wall Street machinery both in connection with reorganizations and new corporate enterprises and consolidations of all kinds.

The Art of Wall Street Investing
By
John Moody

IX

The New York Stock Exchange

NEW YORK has no more entertaining public exhibition than its Stock Exchange. It is one of the show places of the city. The visitor who for the first time looks down from a gallery upon its members in the act of transacting business, is astonished at the apparent confusion he witnesses. He seems to have entered a madhouse. The idea that the market values of our leading securities should be determined by what appears to him to be a howling mob of incurable lunatics, is incomprehensible But if nothing could be said against the Exchange, which is simply a big bazaar for the sale of bonds and stocks, except its tumultuousness and the seeming lack of dignity among its operators, criticism would have in it but an indifferent target for its shafts. Much graver questions

The Art of Wall Street Investing
By
John Moody

grow out of its existence. Is it a harmless institution? Is it a public blessing? Is it a public curse?

As a great central mart for current securities, it is certainly of vast use. There is no reason why bonds and shares should not be publicly dealt in, and in large quantities, as well as dry goods; as well as corn and cotton and beef and kitchen vegetables. If the Stock Exchange transactions were restricted to the bona-fide buying and selling of bonds and shares, not a word could be justly said against it. But is it so restricted? Unfortunately, no. A main occupation is wagering on stocks; many traders while going through the form of buying and selling, simply bet their money upon the rise or fall of the shares they select, as they would upon the shiftings of cards or dice. The Exchange, while doing a large legitimate business, is also an immense speculating establishment.

Its members are divided into two classes — those who execute commissions for others and those who deal on their own account. It is needless

The Art of Wall Street Investing
By
John Moody

to say that among the latter are the boldest and sharpest speculators of the day. The careers of these men can be sketched in very few words. Through the exercise of superior native wits or the accident of extraordinary luck, they flourish marvelously for a time ; but only, as a rule, to lose their heads and their balance at the last and go down, often through a single disastrous transaction — faster than they went up. There are exceptions. Some flourish to the end, dying generally young — or retiring with estates unbroken. But they are exceptions. Wall Street is a place where few fortunes are made and a great many are lost. **The stories of its magnificent triumphs, and of its equally magnificent wrecks, read like tales from "The Arabian Nights"; some of them like passages from "Dante's Inferno."** Wall Street has had its suicides by the dozen, and will have plenty more. It would not be Wall Street without surprises. And yet there is a singular sameness in the ordinary trader's experience. He runs an exciting, if at

The Art of Wall Street Investing
By
John Moody

times a rough and stormy, career,
snatches or seems to snatch a good many
pleasures by the way, makes and breaks
with about equal abandon, wrecks his
health in a hurry, dies early and
suddenly, and then — well, then, when
his affairs come to be settled, there are
often found large blocks of utterly
worthless shares, perhaps a fast horse or
two, possibly a yacht or automobile, some
costly souvenirs, a few solid assets,
possibly heavy debts, or even actual
bankruptcy. Poor fellow, everybody has
forgotten all about him.

Of the ordinary Wall Street
speculator, how- ever clever or however
favored for a time, it is perfectly safe to
say that, if he lives long enough and
sticks to the business, he will finally
come to grief.

**But how about Vanderbilt pere,
who was more or less of a Wall Street
operator all his many days, and a few
others not wholly dissimilar if less
conspicuous examples?**

Ah ! that brings us to a view of some
of the interior workings of the New York

The Art of Wall Street Investing
By
John Moody

Stock Exchange that the public has little conception of, and which alone will give a correct understanding of its real character. The popular idea is that the Exchange has upon its list, to be dealt in, all, or nearly all, prominent stocks and bonds of acknowledged value, impartially selected and solely because of their merits. There could be no greater misconception. We do now always find there the shares of hundreds of high grade securities, both stocks and bonds, representing corporations of high standing, and large business success; railroads, industrials, municipal corporations whose management is unexceptional, and whose securities are among the choicest investments. But if there is a company with a speculative board of directors, and whose stock has been watered until it will float a respectable navy, an attempt is often made to place its shares on the Exchange's list. Or if there is a company that is absolutely controlled and directed by some particularly active and conspicuous manipulator, its stock may

The Art of Wall Street Investing
By
John Moody

often be found at the same place. There
never is, apparently, much difficulty in a
big stock operator getting his issues upon
the list. What has been the result?
Simply that much genuine rubbish has
been unloaded upon the public.

Much, but not too much, has been
said in condemnation of stock watering ;
of the production of corporate securities
representing little or no cash investment,
and which innocent persons are led to
purchase in the belief that they are
getting full values. But how is it that
these speculative issues are so easily
marketed, and the producers escape all
responsibility for the impositions
practiced? Here is where the Exchange's
"credit," so to speak, is often used. The
Exchange is made the conduit through
which the water is diverted to the
investor's pockets. When it takes the
stock upon its list, the Exchange
becomes practically the seller, supplying
the machinery and means of transfer,
and it guarantees nothing. Whoever buys
at its board is understood to take all
risks, no matter how much deception is

The Art of Wall Street Investing
By
John Moody

used. He may be victimized, but he has no redress. The Exchange is simply the medium through which the over-issues have been marketed. It is true, of course, that without the facilities of the Exchange, many of the stock watering frauds which have become historical never could have been successfully consummated.

Once on the Exchange's list, seldom is a stock so worthless that, with a shrewd manipulator behind it, it cannot be at some time unloaded. The process has been a simple one. First they are "washed" — singular how the idea of water runs through all stock operations •—by pre-arranged sales of the stock. Outsiders are then told that there is money in it, and they begin to buy. The stock is duly "supported," an indispensable precaution — that is, it is taken at quotation prices when offered by outside owners, and so up and up it is marked, the speculative public taking large blocks in the belief that it is going higher, and with little thought of its actual value, until there comes a time

The Art of Wall Street Investing
By
John Moody

when the original supply has been exhausted, and the shares are no longer supported, and down, down they go. The real value of the stock has little to do with its negotiations. In the light of this explanation, there is no difficulty in comprehending how certain great financial magnates, who are leading operators in Wall Street, have amassed such colossal fortunes. They have been stock manufacturers as well as stock dealers. The New York Exchange has been their field of operations, their market-place. Through it they have sold their wares. Had they, like ordinary speculators, confined themselves to other people's goods, it is questionable whether they would have grown exceptionally rich. They might have become poor, as most of their associates have done. But when, with consciences conformable to their opportunities, they had the means of selling water at high figures and in practically unlimited quantities, it is no wonder that their fortunes swelled to fabulous proportions. There are many legitimate, lawful and legally controlled

The Art of Wall Street Investing
By
John Moody

exchanges whereon speculation to any
large extent is conducted, but only the
leading ones need be named. The New
York Stock Exchange is a lawfully
constituted association with absolute
power to make and enforce its own rules
and regulations upon its members. An
application for membership in it is
scrutinized with the greatest care, and
the applicant must prove himself to be a
straightforward, honest man before he is
accepted. Transactions between members
are in most instances verbal, and as they
amount to millions of dollars in value
daily, confidence in each other is
imperative. It is a rare occurrence that a
dispute arises, because of the accuracy
and care exercised in transactions with
each other, and, as a rule, the same
honesty and methods are extended to
their relations with customers who are
not members. The legitimate broker is
always solicitous for the welfare of his
client, from selfish motives, if nothing
else. A customer who imagines he has not
been fairly and honestly dealt with has
only to make complaint to the secretary

The Art of Wall Street Investing
By
John Moody

of the Exchange, stating his grievance
and an investigation is had, followed by
redress and the severe discipline of the
offending member, should wrong-doing
be discovered. So high is the character of
the Exchange members that no hesitation
is felt by the public in entrusting to their
custody large sums of money. What is
true of the New York Stock Exchange is
also true of the Chicago Board of Trade,
upon which is handled the vast products
of the great agricultural West. The public
should be warned against speculative
transactions with any but members of
regular exchanges or brokers having
permanent connections with them. The
novice is oftentimes unable to
discriminate between the legitimate and
fraudulent, but there is an infallible test,
as follows: The rules of the New York
Stock Exchange and Chicago Board of
Trade provide that customers shall
receive a memorandum of each
transaction made, which shall show the
date upon which it was made, the price
and with whom, so that if a client has
any doubt about it, he can inquire of the

The Art of Wall Street Investing
By
John Moody

party named on the memorandum whether it is true or not, or he can ask the Secretary of the Exchange to investigate for him. If the Secretary cannot confirm the statements in the memorandum, it often turns out that the parties who are alleged to have participated in the transaction are frauds, masquerading as Stock Exchange members, with whom it is worse than folly to entrust business. Hundreds of them exist in New York City alone, who live as barnacles on the exchanges, bringing ill-fame and discredit to an important business.

It is a common thing for a few large speculators to combine and form a "pool" to advance some specific stock or group of stocks, the idea being that "in union there is strength." In such combinations some one of the members is usually designated as the "manager," who gives all orders for purchase and sale. The business is generally given to a number of commission houses who transact a miscellaneous business, in order to keep the transaction under cover as much as

The Art of Wall Street Investing
By
John Moody

possible, because publicity would probably defeat the plan. The stocks subject to the manipulation are made to look weak and strong alternately — weak in order to induce "short" selling, when the "pool" is a free buyer, and strong to induce "outside" buying when the "pool" is a seller. That part of see-saw manipulation is continued, making the stocks active and attractive to the public, until many thousand shares have been accumulated. In the meantime the most favorable rumors and reports relating to the value of said stocks are carefully put forth through market letters, newspapers, and other well-known mediums. This is done for the purpose of inducing the public to buy, on the perfectly correct theory that the public does buy when it is asked to, providing the price is high and advancing, and especially if it is informed that "strong parties are behind the deal"; when the public "comes in" good and strong, influenced by predictions of a further great advance, it gets the stock. The "strong" parties have "unloaded," the

The Art of Wall Street Investing
By
John Moody

public is "holding the bag" and wonder what is the matter.

Recently a new form of advertising for "lambs" has become popular, which requires no capital beyond the sum needed for newspaper bills. The advertisement usually states that for a small sum, paid "weekly" or "monthly," the subscriber will receive "sure tips" on the market's movements, and that in consideration of one-quarter or one-half of the profits secured, the self-styled "Advisory Brokers" will handle the "deals" for the "lambs" who don't know how to do it for themselves. These "brokers" have a "sure thing," as they always advise one person to operate for the decline and another for an advance. They are certain to make money in one of the transactions. It is marvelous what a number of otherwise cautious, careful people are victimized yearly in these shady operations.

But the Exchange is nevertheless very useful and necessary in supplying quotable values and furnishing a ready market for all classes of securities. This

The Art of Wall Street Investing
By
John Moody

important function of the Exchange is
well brought out in a paragraph taken
from Chas. A. Conant's recently
published book, "Wall Street and the
Country."
Says Mr. Conant:

"One of the most persistent of the
hallucinations which prevail among
people otherwise apparently lucid and
well informed, is the conception that
operations on stock and produce
exchanges are pure gambling. A
moment's reflection, it would seem, might
convince such persons that a function
which occupies so important a place in
the mechanism of modern business must
be a useful and necessary part of that
mechanism; but reflection seems to have
little part in the intellectual equipment of
the assailants of organized markets. Only
recently I picked up a book purporting to
treat of the subject of ethics, and found
this remarkable passage: "If, instead of
betting on something so small as falling
dice, one bets on the rise and fall of
stocks or on the price which wheat will

The Art of Wall Street Investing
By
John Moody

reach some months hence, and if by such betting one corners the community in an article essential to its welfare, throwing a continent into confusion, the law will pay not the slightest attention. A gambling house for these larger purposes may be built conspicuously in any city, the sign "Stock Exchange" be set over its door, influential men appointed its officers, and the law will protect it and them as it does the churches. How infamous to forbid gambling on a small scale and almost to encourage it on a large!'

"The writer who undertook to discuss the Stock Exchange in that manner in a book on ethics, might well have devoted himself less earnestly to the smaller refinements of ethical definition and reverted to the ancient maxim, 'Thou shalt not bear false witness against thy neighbor.' What he says is a hodgepodge of misconceptions. If it be true that betting on the rise and fall of stocks be gambling, as it undoubtedly is, then what follows has no relation to the first suggestion. To one having any knowledge of the subject-matter the two

The Art of Wall Street Investing
By
John Moody

parts of the first sentence are
inconsistent with each other and
mutually destructive. Pure betting is done
in bucket-shops, is of no use to the
community, is destructive to the morals
and pockets of young men, and cannot be
too severely censured. But such betting is
not confined to buildings bearing the sign
'Stock Exchange.' It has nothing to do
with the legitimate processes of the
exchanges. Moreover, one cannot corner
the community on any 'article essential to
its welfare' by betting in bucket-shops.
He may perhaps do it within certain
limits by actual transactions on the
produce exchanges, because they involve
the right to demand delivery. If it were
true, however, that no such deliveries
were contemplated or could be made, as
is usually the case in bucket-shop
gambling, it would no more be possible to
corner the supply of wheat by betting on
its future price than it is possible for a
politician to carry the election his way by
laying heavy odds on his candidate. His
bets would not make votes, and merely

The Art of Wall Street Investing
By
John Moody

betting on the prices of the commodity
would not influence the supply.

"The fact that such confusion of
ideas prevails, and that the Stock and
Produce exchanges continue to be looked
upon by many good people as a sort of
adjunct of Monte Carlo, justifies an
occasional restatement of in the
mechanism of business. To take the
subject up from an elementary
standpoint, it is well to say a word
regarding the function of stock
companies. The discovery was made long
before our time that a piece of property or
a new enterprise could be given mobility
and divisibility by putting the title to its
ownership into transferable shares. The
creation of share companies enables the
small capital of the essential part which
these exchanges play individuals to be
gathered into large funds necessary to
build factories and railways. It divides the
risk of an undertaking among many
persons, and places the enterprise
beyond the accidents of a single human
existence by giving it a fictitious body
dowered by law with perpetual life."

The Art of Wall Street Investing
By
John Moody

But in addition to being a balance-wheel to the business of the country, Stock Exchange speculation is often a disturbing factor. It does not even furnish trustworthy news. Nowhere is it so difficult to get reliable intelligence concerning any stock dealt in there, as in Wall Street. The inventiveness of the speculative broker is something marvelous. He can ruin the country one hour and save it the next. He can blight the crops of a whole section, or he can fill the land with abundance. He can make war or he can make peace, exactly as his monetary interest demands. Rumor-mongering seems to be a part of his trade. He is the chief of liars. Perhaps he is the exception rather than the rule among his fellows— it is to be hoped that he is — but he is a pretty numerous exception, for all that! What is the consequence? Simply that when a financial storm threatens the country, the Exchange is almost certain to be the center of disturbance. No other institution is so sensitive. It exaggerates all the symptoms of trouble. It sends out

The Art of Wall Street Investing
By
John Moody

its alarming reports as the storm-cloud
sends out its lightning. Looking at it as
the barometer of values, the timid
naturally conclude that everything is lost,
and thus the evil is unduly magnified.
Wall Street is as much the natural field
for panics as the prairie is for tornadoes.

While the Exchange has been of
advantage to the business interests of the
country, there are many who have had
dealings with it who would not testify in
its favor. Of the thousands and
thousands who have visited it in person
or by proxy, and done a little business
with it, not many are ready to rise up and
call it blessed, except in a qualified sense.
If all were to give their experiences, what
would the verdict be? It is to be
apprehended that the evidence of a very
decided majority would not be flattering
to Wall Street's speculative methods; that
their testimony would be that they had
found it easier to lose money than to
make it.

The man who says he "never
speculates in stocks, but buys only what
he can pay for," is a sufferer as frequently

The Art of Wall Street Investing
By
John Moody

as the man who buys on a "margin." He is
generally a "sticker" — one who never
"lets go." He buys a security that he
believes in, and so strong is his
confidence that he will not accept a
generous profit if it is offered him, and he
is still more tenacious when a loss is
growing. His temperament will not admit
of the possibility of an eventual loss, but
the rule (with the exceptions) is that he
will finally take his loss when it has
reached its greatest proportions.
Securities amounting to hundreds of
millions of dollars have been carried by
people who "never speculate," through
the depression of the past four years.
They have paid interest on money
borrowed, paid assessments under
reorganization schemes, and still a loss
stares them in the face.

X

Wall Street Phrases and Methods

IN the Wall Street field many terms and phrases are used which are not familiar to the outsider and therefore require definition in a book of this kind. In fact, many practical Wall Street people, while clearly understanding the meaning of such and such a phrase or word, cannot always concisely define it, or convey its exact meaning to the inquirer. In the following pages the chief terms and phrases relating to the modes and general mechanism of the Street are briefly defined and explained. The various words or phrases are taken up in alphabetical order.

Arbitrage. The buying and selling of the same security in different markets, as New York and London, or New York and

The Art of Wall Street Investing
By
John Moody

Chicago, for the purpose of making a profit from the difference in quotation between the two markets. This trading is of course based on temporary differences in prices between the markets, which are due from some special cause. If all things were equal every stock would, of course, have the same value in every market in which it is dealt in. There are two kinds of arbitrage dealings in stocks between New York and London. One operation is known as the "spread" and the other the "back-spread."

Averaging. This is a speculative term which is used to describe purchases or sales of stock which are made when the market is rising or falling, as the case may be, for the purpose of improving the position of the buyer or seller in the matter of his average price for all his securities. For instance, if 100 shares are purchased at 95 and the price declines to 75, the averager will purchase another hundred shares at 75, thus bringing the average cost of his total holdings to 85. Hence, as soon as the price of the stock recovers to over 85 he will have a profit on his entire transactions.

Bear. This is the name for a speculator who sells stock short in expectation of buying it back at a lower price. In order to do this he of course borrows a certificate to deliver against his sale, and when he has bought in or "covered" he uses the new bought certificate to repay the loaner.

Bill of Exchange. This is a written order or request from one person to another for pay-merit to a third party, the amount paid being charged to the one who issues or signs the bill. There is in reality no difference between a "bill of exchange" and an ordinary draft, but the former term is commonly applied to an order for money payable in a foreign country, whereas the same sort of order payable within the country of its origin is known as a "draft."

Blind Pool. A blind pool in the stock market is one where the members join together and contribute capital, agreeing that only the manager shall have full charge of the pool and know in what way

The Art of Wall Street Investing
By
John Moody

the money is to be used. Blind pools are not confined to stocks but may be carried on in a scheme of almost any nature.

Bobtail Pool. This is a term which usually applies to a small or informal pool in stocks. In such cases the members join together to move the stock either up or down and then each is usually allowed to suit his own pleasure in closing out his interest in the pool.

Bucketing. This is a term used to describe sales made by a broker for his own account and risk against customers" purchases or purchases by the broker against customers' sales. It is a reprehensible practice and is usually done to enable the broker to speculate against his customers' trades. In such instances the broker wins if his customers lose, or he loses if his customers win.

Bucket Shop. This is a place usually advertised as a brokerage office where bets are made on regular stock exchange quotations. No actual transactions take place. Usually money is put up by the customer and a commission is charged

The Art of Wall Street Investing
By
John Moody

for buying and selling the same as on a regular exchange. When the quotations show a profit to the customer, he is privileged to demand his profit ; when the limit of the customer's margin has been reached in the price of the stock, the customer has lost his bet and his money and is "wiped out."

Call. A call on a stock is a contract or agreement binding the issuer to deliver to the holder of the call the stock named therein within a certain time, at a certain price, if the holder shall so demand. For instance, the one issuing a call will agree to deliver one hundred shares of a specified stock within thirty days at 110 if the purchaser makes a demand for it. Should the stock be selling at 106 the issuer of the call may be able to sell his promise for $100. The purchaser of the call will then hold the same, and if the stock rises above in within the thirty days he will call upon the issuer for the hundred shares at 110 and probably sell the same in the market at or over 111, thus realizing a profit. A contract of the

The Art of Wall Street Investing
By
John Moody

same kind applying to the short side of the market is known as a "put."

Corner. A corner in a stock is caused by the purchase by a pool or other interest of all the floating or purchasable stock of the company, after which the price can be advanced at the will of those creating the corner. Speculators who are short of the stock and are unable to buy or borrow to make delivery or return stock which they have borrowed, are thus forced into a corner and "squeezed." They must settle with the buyers at the buyers' own prices.
Covering. This is a term used in the stock market to describe the act of buying stocks or commodities for the purpose of closing short contracts, that is to say, buying back stocks previously sold but which were not possessed when sold.
Due Bill. In stock exchange parlance a due bill is a promise to pay a dividend which has been declared but has not yet been paid by the company. For instance, a stock certificate may be purchased in the market after the transfer books of the

The Art of Wall Street Investing
By
John Moody

corporation have been closed, or the transfer of the stocks may not have been made, but by agreement the dividend is to go to the purchaser, and not to the party in whose name the certificate stands. When the dividend is paid to the original party the due bill is presented to him and he passes the dividend over to the purchaser.

Ex-dividend. When a stock upon which a dividend has been declared is sold and the price is not to include the amount of the dividend to be shortly paid, the stock is said to be sold "ex-dividend."

Flat. This signifies "without interest." When bonds are sold flat no charge is made to the buyer for the accrued interest, as the interest is included in the price of the bond. On the New York Stock Exchange all bonds are sold at "flat" prices, but in private transactions a large majority of the sales are made on an "accrued interest" basis. The term "flat" is also used in relation to the lending of stocks. When stocks are lent flat the lender does not pay interest to the borrower of this stock. Otherwise the

The Art of Wall Street Investing
By
John Moody

borrower will pay the lender the market value of the stock and the lender will pay interest to the borrower on his money.

Giving up. This term is used in the stock markets to describe a broker who executes an order for another broker and whose connection with the transaction then ends. In reporting to the broker to whom he sells or from whom he buys the name of the broker for whom he is acting, he is said to "give up" the latter. The latter receives the stock and completes the transaction.

Hypothecation. This signifies the pledging of securities or other property as collateral for loans. In Wall Street, where stocks are purchased on margin and carried by a broker for his customer, they are usually hypothecated or deposited as collateral in loans with banks or trust companies or other loaners of money. It is in this way that the broker secures the capital to carry the stocks for his customer.

Irish Dividend. This is a term sometimes used to describe not a dividend, but an assessment on a stock.

The Art of Wall Street Investing
By
John Moody

Joint Account. The term for a transaction in which two or more brokers or speculators join together for their mutual benefit or risk in the carrying through of a transaction.

Long of stocks. This is the phrase used when a speculator is a bull ; that is to say when his account shows a balance of stocks on the long or bull side. The opposite condition is to be short of stocks and be on the bear side.

Manipulation. This word applies to the operation of working stocks both up and down on the exchanges, both ways at once. A well-known method of manipulating a stock is to put through on the exchange a number of fictitious sales, one broker agreeing to purchase at a certain price from another and the latter then agreeing to repurchase the same stock at the same or another price. This arrangement is sometimes carried on between various brokers, each transaction being offset in some way by another. As a result there may be a large number of quotations reported with no actual sales. These quotations are

The Art of Wall Street Investing
By
John Moody

commonly known as "wash" transactions, and the purpose usually is to create outside interest in the stock and start a speculation in it among genuine buyers and sellers.

Margin. This is the word used to describe money deposited with a broker for speculation in stocks, grain or other commodities. In stocks the margin required ranges from 5% to 30%, dependent upon the character of the security purchased. The average margin is 10%, which amounts to $1,000 on the ordinary one hundred shares of stock. The margin protects the customer down to a price ten points below the price he has paid, if he is long of stock, and ten points above the price he has received if he is short of the stock. As his margin becomes narrower because of the change in the market prices he is required to put up more money or else have his account closed out.

Outside broker. This term describes a broker who is not a member of the regular exchange, but who deals in securities either on the streets or

The Art of Wall Street Investing
By
John Moody

elsewhere. In New York City an outside broker is one who deals in what is known as the outside market or on the curb. There are nowadays a very large number of stocks and bonds which are traded in in this outside market, and these outside brokers usually conduct just as legitimate a business as those who make trades on the stock exchange.

Passing a dividend. This does not mean declaring a dividend, as many people assume, but it means failure to declare a dividend that had previously been regularly paid. When the company specifically states that it will not pay a similar dividend to that which previously had been paid, then it is said that the dividend is stopped. But when no official action is taken and the dividend simply is not declared by the directors, it is said to have been "passed."

Privilege. This is a general name for a call, a put, a spread or a straddle, information as to each of these terms being supplied under their own headings. In any kind of a privilege the purchaser of

The Art of Wall Street Investing
By
John Moody

the same is not liable for loss beyond the amount actually paid for it.

Put. A put on a stock is the reverse of a call, being a written contract or agreement binding the issuer to receive from the holder the stock named in the agreement within a certain time at a certain price if the holder shall so demand. The act of delivering such stock to the issuer of the contract is generally known as "putting" the stock.

Pyramiding. This describes operations by the use of paper profits made in transactions not yet closed and, therefore, not yet in hand. For instance, one may purchase one hundred shares of stock at 50 on a margin of 10% of the par value. If the stock advances to 60 the purchaser will then have 20% margin and he will purchase one hundred shares more. If the price then goes to 70 he will purchase two hundred shares more, giving him four hundred in all. If it next goes to 80 he will then purchase four hundred shares more, giving him eight hundred shares in all, on which he has a margin of 10%, or $8,ooo» Up to this

The Art of Wall Street Investing
By
John Moody

point his paper profits will be $7,000. If the market continues in its rise he will continue accumulating stock, until his account shows very large accumulated paper profits. If he then sells out he will have turned his profits into cash, but if the market suddenly drops ten points he will not only have lost the profit on the last transaction, but will have lost everything. In other words, the inverted pyramid will have fallen and ruined him in the crash.

Spread. A spread is a put and call combined and is practically the same as a straddle. If the stock goes below the price named in the put end, plus the cost of the spread, the holder makes a profit; also if the stock goes above the price named in the call end, plus the cost of the spread, the holder of the spread also profits. In other words, the purchaser of a spread is said to "play the two ends against the middle"; he has two chances to make money and his loss in any case is limited to the cost of the spread.

Straddle. A straddle is similar to a spread with the exception that only one

The Art of Wall Street Investing
By
John Moody

price is named in it. The stock may be called for or delivered at this one price only. As in the other cases, the stock must go up or down more than the amount paid for the straddle before there is a profit in it.

Under the rule. This is a term used to describe an official transaction made on the New York Stock Exchange. In case a member of the Exchange fails to receive or deliver stock in accordance with his contract of purchase or sale, the stock in question is bought or sold, as the case may be, by the chairman of the Exchange for the account of the delinquent member, and any difference in cost is charged or credited to him. When transactions of this kind are put through they are known as purchases or sales made "under the rule."

Washing. This term describes the operation of simultaneous buying and selling the same stocks for the purpose of making quotations and inducing outside speculation or interest in the stock by imparting apparent activity to it. Washing

The Art of Wall Street Investing
By
John Moody

is usually employed when manipulation of some kind is in progress.

Watered stock. A term used to describe the capital stock of a company which is not supposed to be represented with a corresponding amount of assets. The term as used is a vague one and is subject to several interpretations. For instance, when a stock dividend is declared the original stock is said to be watered to that extent, unless the newly issued stock represents added property or value in some form.

The Art of Wall Street Investing
By
John Moody

CONCLUSION

In Wall Street no one is always right ; cheap advice is plentiful; some men learn only by failing; losses make us more cautious; interrogate before you negotiate; money is most valued when lost; don't buy an egg until it is laid ; fraud is built on misrepresentation ; speculation begins when certainty ends; opportunity is often lost by deliberating; get information before you invest, not after; get an investment that will let you sleep ; it is idle to wait for your ship to come in unless you have sent one out; those who lament their misfortunes are generally they who do not recognize their opportunities; buyers of stock belong to two classes: those who trade on tendencies and who take hold wherever the market is active without much reference to values or prices, and those who always try to buy when prices are down instead of when they are up.

In Wall Street the investor determines the prices of stocks in the long run. This

The Art of Wall Street Investing
By
John Moody

statement is sometimes disputed by those who point to the fluctuations which are confessedly made by manipulators without regard to value. It is true that such fluctuations do occur, but when the manipulation is over the influence of the investor is again felt. If he decides that a given stock is worth only so much the manipulator will ultimately be compelled to accept that valuation, because manipulation cannot be kept up. The general object of manipulation is to buy below value and sell above value.

"An important influence of the stock exchanges, and in some ways also of the produce exchanges, is the influence they exert upon the money market. The possession by any country of a large mass of salable securities affords a powerful guarantee against the effects of a severe money panic. If in New York there arises a sudden pressure of money, so that confidence becomes impaired and people having contracts entitling to future or immediate delivery of money insist that these contracts shall be executed in money instead of other forms of promises,

The Art of Wall Street Investing
By
John Moody

what happens? The banks call in loans and begin to hold their cash. If they hold large quantities of securities salable on the London, Paris or Berlin market a cable order will affect the sale of these in an hour, and the gold proceeds will be on their way across the Atlantic in a day.

"Wonderful has been the effect within the last twenty-five years of this steady influence of the stock market upon the demand for money and upon the smoothness of the operations of the mechanism of the exchanges. What has just been put in a crude form by referring to a crisis occurs daily and hourly on the stock exchanges, and prevents sudden contraction and expansion in the rate for loans. The manufacturer goes placidly on paying his four or five per cent, for commercial loans, when if there were no stock exchanges where securities could be sold in one market at a slight profit over another, he would find that his bank was first charging seven or eight percent., then dropping to three or four and then going back to eight. By means of the facilities which the stock market affords

The Art of Wall Street Investing
By
John Moody

for placing credit instantly at the command of one market or another the pressure for money is mitigated, and has put a limited effect upon the commercial borrower. Such pressure as now occurs is transferred to the borrower on call — the broker in stocks, who thus acts as insurer for the commercial borrower. This influence of the stock market has much the effect of a buffer upon the impact of two solid bodies. Crises are prevented when they can be prevented, and when they cannot they are anticipated, and their force is broken into a mild succession of ripples instead of a tidal wave."— Chas. A. Conant, "Wall Street and the Country."

The Art of Wall Street Investing
By
John Moody

"A man's learning dies with him; even his virtues fade out of remembrance; out the dividends on the stocks he bequeaths to his children live and keep his memory green."
— Holmes.

The Art of Wall Street Investing
By
John Moody

NOTES

The Art of Wall Street Investing
By
John Moody

NOTES

The Art of Wall Street Investing
By
John Moody

NOTES

The Art of Wall Street Investing
By
John Moody

NOTES

The Art of Wall Street Investing
By
John Moody

NOTES

NOTES

The Art of Wall Street Investing
By
John Moody

NOTES

The Art of Wall Street Investing
By
John Moody

NOTES

The Art of Wall Street Investing
By
John Moody

NOTES

The Art of Wall Street Investing
By
John Moody

NOTES